MRS Rekhr

G000144633

THE CROCODILE'S Teeth

TRADING, TYRANNY & TERRORISM ON TWO CONTINENTS

SAM THAKER

THE CROCODILE'S Teeth

Edited by Chris Newton

MEMOIRS
Cirencester

Published by Memoirs

MEMOIRS

Memoirs Books

25 Market Place, Cirencester, Gloucestershire, GL7 2NX
info@memoirsbooks.co.uk www.memoirsbooks.co.uk

Copyright ©Sam Thaker, August 2011
First published in England, August 2011
Book jacket design Ray Lipscombe

ISBN 978-1-908223-23-4

All rights reserved.

No part of this publication may be reproduced, stored in a retrieval system, or transmitted
in any form or by any means, electronic, mechanical, photocopying, recording or otherwise
without the prior permission of Memoirs.

Printed in England

CONTENTS

A message of inspiration

At the age of ten I became an adult. The curse of poverty hindered my education, but when I grew up, determination brought me success.

The Uganda where I was born in 1940 was a peaceful and wonderful country, a paradise. And then, overnight, the dream was shattered by the brutal dictatorship of Idi Amin. I had to run for my life. I lost everything I had, except my determination to succeed.

As a refugee in England I had to overcome cultural barriers and hardship to become a part of English society. In India I not only had to overcome more cultural barriers but endure catastrophic flood and terrorist attack, yet once again I achieved success through sheer determination.

Today my wife and I are happily retired and living in England, but the memories of what I went through will never leave me.

I believe people of all ages will enjoy reading my story. More than this, I hope it will bring inspiration. I am an ordinary man, yet three times I rose from being a penniless immigrant to achieve success. If I can do it, so can you.

Sam Thaker
August 2011

E-mail: crockteethsam@yahoo.com

Dedication

This book is dedicated to my late mother, Hemkuvar, and to my beloved wife Ranjna. So much would have been impossible without them.

INTRODUCTION

When we are among friends for a casual get-together or chatting over dinner in a quiet restaurant, we often start talking about our personal experiences. If the subject is interesting, most of us will listen, storing up what they are being told. I have done it myself many times, perhaps to quote an example for a point I'm trying to make, or just to get a laugh.

My story is a little different from most, because I was born and brought up in Uganda in East Africa. When I start to talk about my homeland, I immediately see the curiosity on people's faces. To many people Africa is still an unknown country.

As most Westerners will remember, Uganda was devastated in the 1970s by the terrible effects of the Idi Amin régime, and most of the Asian community of which I was a member were forced to flee the country, despite having become the backbone of the Ugandan economy. I saw all this at first hand and was a victim myself.

Some friends who have heard my story have told me it is extraordinary. "You should write a book about it!" they say. Even my son and my wife tell me I should put my experiences into words. For a long time I never thought seriously of doing such a thing, as I took what had happened to me for granted. I felt I had lived an ordinary life, just like everybody else.

Then when I thought about it I began to realise that perhaps my experiences of those times really were interesting enough to be made into a story. In fact it occurred to me that some of the events were so extraordinary that people would think I had made them up. My friends and family told me not to worry about that.

It was an incident that happened on a trip to Germany that made my mind up for me. For the last five years my wife and I have been going there every year so that she can have homeopathy and naturopathy treatment. We visit a small town called Markdorf in Southern Germany, very close to Lake Constance. Lake Constance is shared between Switzerland, Germany and Austria. Markdorf is a beautiful town and on a clear day you can see the Swiss Alps.

In 2008 we had some friends from Canada with us. They were visiting Markdorf because we had recommended our doctor to them. It was a weekend, so we all decided to take a train and go sightseeing. As we waited in the station, a young German came up and started talking to me. He spoke very good English. He was curious as to where I came from, because you don't see many tourists in Markdorf. He was very interested to hear that I had been born in Africa. We chatted casually, and I told him about Idi Amin and how his régime had led to us leaving Uganda.

We were still talking away on the platform when the train came. This young man was catching the same train. He asked if he could sit with us and hear more of my story, and I was happy to oblige. We were heading for the sixth stop after Markdorf. He was getting off at the third, but when the train reached his stop, he stayed on it.

The young man continued listening with great interest as I told him what had happened in Uganda. When I said I was planning to write a book, he urged me to make sure it was translated into German, as he thought many of his countrymen would be interested in reading my story. He came all the way with us to our stop, then got off with us and took the train back home.

In the years when I was running my own business I was too busy to think about writing down all the things that happened to me, but now I am retired and have more time, I have decided to commit my experiences to paper. I hope you find my story as interesting as that young man did.

CHAPTER 1

EAST AFRICA: LAND OF OPPORTUNITY

Let me begin by giving you a glimpse of my father's background. Balkrishna Thaker was born in 1890 in Gujarat, India, during the years of the British Raj. My grandfather Ramji was a police inspector in a small town called Garamli, and in addition to my father he had two other sons and a daughter. As a police officer he imposed strict discipline on his children.

My father, by contrast, was totally undisciplined and very mischievous. They did not get along as a good father-and-son team. My father could not tolerate his father's strictness and the constant differences of opinion between them.

One day when he was 18 years old, my father ran away to Karachi with a friend. He somehow got a job there as a teacher, but unfortunately the job did not last very long. He could not make a living in Karachi, so he had no choice but to go back to his family in Gujarat. As they were living in a very small town where the economy depended mainly on farming, opportunities were limited.

One day in 1911 as my father was strolling in the bazaar, he heard the beating of drums. A man was making an announcement on behalf of the British Government in India. He said there was a great opportunity for anyone wanting to migrate to East Africa – they would be given a free passage to start a new life. East Africa too was ruled by the British Government. There was no need for a passport, and a free passage would be provided, along with some money.

It seemed that the Government needed skilled people to build a railway in East Africa and were looking for traders, builders and so on. The purpose of bringing people to East Africa was to build a whole new world there, so all sorts of people with various trades and abilities were needed.

My father was very excited when he heard this announcement, and immediately put himself on the list. After a few days he was called to the Government office, where he was accepted for a free passage. In addition to this he was given an umbrella, a coconut and five rupees to spend when he got there – at that time the currency in East Africa was Indian rupees.

My grandfather objected to all this very strongly. He did not want his son to leave home and travel to Africa. But my dad was stubborn, as usual, and his father could not stop him.

My father boarded a sailing boat in Bombay for the 3000-mile sea crossing. This was the first time he had ever left India or gone on such a long journey. After a voyage of many days he arrived in the port of Mombasa, in Kenya. In those days Kenya was a British colony, Uganda a protectorate and Tanganyika a territory, and they were all considered to belong to one country, East Africa. Kenya and Tanganyika were on the Indian Ocean, while Uganda was inland and bordered by Sudan, Congo and Rwanda as well as Kenya and Tanganyika.

The railway service was already running from Mombasa to Kampala, the biggest city in Uganda and today its capital. The trains were always full of Indian labourers going to Uganda to build more railway tracks, along with traders and other people embarking on a new life.

The train journey was a dangerous one, as it travelled through the unknown. There was a great fear of wild animals attacking people working in the open fields. Malaria, blackwater fever and yellow fever were then killer diseases, and there were no medicines or doctors. Housing conditions for the railway workers were very poor.

My father knew all this, but he still decided to go on into the East African interior. He had some contacts in Kampala who had arrived there earlier.

It was December, and very hot. The journey was about 800 miles and the railway ran through thick jungle, with tall trees and dense bushes. In many places the jungle was so thick that no sunlight could get through.

After travelling for few days my father arrived in Kampala. He found the country very green, with rich vegetation and a moderate climate. In fact, he found himself in an East African paradise.

Kampala stands right on the equator, but it is 1200m above sea level, so it is not excessively hot. It is built on a series of hills, like a miniature San Francisco. The original city was built on a hill called Mengo, where the kabaka, the king, was living. In this area there used to be many impala, a species of antelope - the name Kampala comes from that word.

My father's contacts in Uganda advised him to open a shop, as they already had their own shops selling food, clothes and other merchandise for the daily consumption. My dad had very little money, but his relatives helped him by giving him some merchandise to get the business started and allowing him to pay them back later.

They had already created a small village, called Katera, and were living and working next to each other. There was no electricity and they were allowed to keep guns for their protection. At night they would take it in turn to stay awake guarding their homes against wild animals. The buildings were mainly made of corrugated iron sheets, as this was the quickest way to put a roof over your head. The shops were in front and the living accommodation at the back. The nights would often seem very long, as there was a continuous noise of wild animals, but fortunately no-one was attacked.

My dad began to do reasonably well selling general merchandise like food and clothes. There was a continuous flow of new immigrants arriving from India. The Indian community who were already settled in Uganda were extending their help to the new and needy immigrants by building houses and shops, letting them have merchandise on loan (there were no banks) to run the shops and giving them money to start new businesses like farming, workshops and vehicle repair garages, purely on a trust basis. Most of the merchandise was imported from England. Trust played a great part in their lives. Money was borrowed by one from another purely on word of mouth, and there were no written agreements. Each transaction was honoured. This amazing spirit of unity and co-operation soon brought huge success to the people and their new country.

As my father was now settling down, he decided to go back to India and get married. He got married in Gujarat and brought his new wife, my stepmother, to Africa. After a couple of years they had a son, whom they called Bachu.

Unfortunately my stepmother died of malaria when she was still very young. After his wife died it was very difficult for my father to run the business and look after Bachu as well. His relatives offered to help look after the boy, but it was still difficult for my dad to manage all this, so he decided to go back to India and get married again. He brought his new wife, Hemkuvar, my mother, back to Africa and they continued their new life in Katera.

In 1933 my older brother Shashi was born, then two years later Arvind. Bachu joined the British Army. As there were no schools in Katera, my parents sent Shashi and Arvind to Jinja, Uganda's second largest town to the north east of Kampala, which was then the capital of Busoga Kingdom (Jinja means stone in Swahili). The town is on the shores of Lake Victoria, the biggest lake in the world apart from Lake Superior in Canada, and the River Nile has its source there.

It was common for people to travel from one place to another in search of success and to make their home in any new town where there were good prospects. My father travelled to many towns, one of which was Masindi, where I was born in 1940.

Masindi was a very small village with no school or hospital, while Jinja was a fair-sized town with a nice school. My two brothers were living there with a family known to my father, so Dad was looking for an opportunity to move there as well. Fortunately he got a chance to do business in Jinja, and in 1942 he moved there. He purchased a truck and started a transport business. He was transporting logs from the jungle and taking them to a sawmill to be cut into timber for building and so on. His youngest son, Manu, was born in Jinja in 1944.

The continuous growth of the business network in East Africa soon warranted a new currency, the East African shilling. There were 20 shillings to one pound sterling, as in Britain at the time. The roads and other infrastructure improved and for everyone life got better and better, particularly compared with the hardship they had known in the past.

Schools and hospitals were set up in the big towns, and the town of Kampala was growing like wildfire. It had the world-class Makerere University and a big hospital, Mulago Hospital, both of which became landmarks. Many great African politicians came to Makerere University from various parts of Africa to be educated. Thing were going well for Uganda and for my father.

CHAPTER TWO

SCHOOLDAYS AND STRANGE PETS

I started my education in the Government Primary School in Jinja. My father, mother, brothers and I shared a nice house. Behind the house there was a small compound with high walls around it for security and a small gate for us to get in and out.

Our house was opposite Uganda House, a Ford dealership. I had two very good school friends, and the three of us were always playing badminton at the side of our house or cricket on the public sports ground. My younger brother Manu always wanted to tag along with us. We did not want him to play with us because he was not as old as we were, yet somehow he would manage to push his way into coming with us wherever we went.

Sometimes we would go for a walk to the Rippon Falls, the source of the White Nile, one of the main tributaries of the Nile. The water cascades down from Lake Victoria with great force, thundering into the river. Next to the falls there was a little 30-yard strip of land which divided the great falls and their white water from an area of deep, slow-flowing water away from the main river. There was an old building here on two floors, a disused pumping station. It had a terrace overlooking the bank on the quiet side of the river. We would enjoy going there and sitting on the edge of the terrace watching the foaming white water to one side and the deep blue water merging into the main river on the other.

One hot Sunday, the temptation to jump into the quiet water for a dip was particularly strong. None of us could swim, but that was all the more reason for us to learn. However, we knew there were crocodiles. From the top of the terrace we could sometimes see them in the blue water, and some of them were huge. Even so, we were determined to learn to swim in the river.

We thought of a clever idea — we would throw stones in to drive the crocodiles away. We threw a few stones, then we jumped into the shallow part of the river. We felt very excited about our adventure, but we were also very scared of the crocodiles.

I was more scared of the crocodiles than my friends were. I was also very scared of snakes as well, particularly the black mamba, so I tried to persuade them not to go into the river. They argued with me and convinced me in the end, and I was persuaded to join them.

Of course there was no coach to teach us swimming, so we had to teach ourselves. We were soon swimming regularly in the river, always throwing stones in first to scare away the crocodiles. As we were now becoming expert swimmers, we started jumping into the water from the terrace.

The four of us promised each other that we would never tell our parents about our swimming, because we knew that if we did they would scold us and forbid us to go to the river. We didn't tell our school friends about our secret place, either. But we could not keep the secret from them for long. Some boys started bragging about how clever and brave they had been. As a result many more boys started coming to the river for a swim. We ended up having 15 other boys all swimming with us. Fortunately, the crocodiles stayed away.

The area where we swam was slow-moving and calm, slowly getting faster as it flowed into the main river. Some of the braver boys started getting adventurous. They said the area we were swimming in was too small and we should go further, into the fast-moving part of the river. Many of us argued that they were not prepared to swim in the faster-moving water, as it was dangerous, but some of the older boys were determined. Two of them in particular did not want to lose face, so they started swimming in the faster water. They began bragging about their achievement to the rest of us and persuaded some of the other boys to join them in this wild adventure. We didn't agree with this as we felt it was our place, and they were taking it over. This put us off going to the river, and we started going less often.

One day at school we heard that one of our friends had drowned in the river. We asked the other boys what had happened. They had found his body by the riverbank, not far from the place where we had been swimming.

After this incident, we all stopped going. I felt very guilty, as we were the ones who had started this wild adventure. Night after night I would have nightmares, seeing myself drowning and choking in the river. I used to get up in the middle of the night and think about my friend who had died. After this incident my mother asked me if I was going to the Nile to swim too, but I said I was not going.

My father was kept very busy with his transport business. One day while he was driving his truck in the jungle, he found a little spotted kitten which seemed very lost and was struggling to walk. There was no-one around and the kitten was crying. My dad felt sorry for it and brought it home. We gave it some milk in a saucer.

We already had a dog, a cat, a parrot and a monkey in the house. The dog was called Poppy, the cat Tom, the parrot Kasuku (Swahili for parrot) and the monkey was called Mickey. The little spotted kitten was very much welcomed by everyone in our home, including Poppy, Tom and Mickey. We called him Raja.

As the days went past, Raja just kept on growing. We soon realised that he was not a domestic cat, but a leopard. Within a short time he was already larger than a domestic cat.

Raja was soon our best friend, and he was especially close to me. I used to play with Raja and Poppy in our compound by throwing a rubber ball for both Raja and Poppy. Raja use to growl and Poppy barked when they were both running to fetch the ball. Raja was aggressive and bullied Poppy. When he growled at Poppy the dog would back off with his tail between his legs.

Unfortunately there was a problem with having Raja in our home. The news quickly spread to the rest of the neighbourhood that we had a chui

(Swahili for leopard), and the milkman, vegetable sellers and other suppliers refused to deliver to us any more. The good news was that we were absolutely safe from being robbed, as no burglars would come anywhere near.

One day I was ill with a very high temperature and had a severe chill. My father called the doctor. I had a blanket over me, and Raja as usual was asleep with me under my blanket.

The doctor sat on the edge of my bed and examined me. He said I had malaria, but it was nothing to worry about as it was curable. He said he would give me an injection in my bottom. He pulled back the blanket, and out sprang Raja.

The doctor was petrified. His jaw dropped and he froze. He dropped his bag on my bed and ran to his car. I was very surprised at this response, because it was only my little Raja in the bed.

My dad went to the car and asked the doctor why he had run away. The doctor was very angry.

"You people are mad!" he said. "You're living in a zoo full of wild animals. If you need treatment from me you'll have to come to my surgery. Please bring me my bag!" My dad got the bag from the bed and gave it back to the doctor.

So after that my father had to take me to the doctor for treatment. I got better after a few days.

We had a lot of fun with our pets. Kasuku the parrot picked up quite a few words from us, and he could also bark like Poppy, so as you can imagine our home was very noisy. My friends used to come round because they liked playing with our pets.

Mickey the monkey had a leather belt round his waist. There was a chain tied to the belt, and the other end was tied to a ladder leaning against the wall. That allowed Mickey to sit on one of the steps and swing through the air.

Almost every day we would see the same little drama. Tom the cat would walk towards the ladder, his tail upright like an aerial. Mickey would wait in great excitement, screaming and swinging through the air. Kasuku did not want to miss out either, and he would start barking like the dog. My friends and I would run in to watch, because we knew what was going to happen and wanted to see it.

As Tom approached, Mickey would start swinging until he could reach down to him, catch hold of his tail and swing the poor cat up into the air. Tom would get furious and try to attack him with his claws, but Mickey was very quick and would throw Tom back to the floor before he could make contact.

We used to scream with laughter at Tom's stupidity. He didn't need to go under the ladder, why didn't he go a different way? I always wondered why he didn't work that out. But it was great fun to watch.

One day my father came to talk to us children. He was looking sad and worried. He started talking in a low, emotional voice. He said he had been called by the doctor and told that keeping our leopard was too dangerous. You were allowed to keep wild animals in the house only if they were controllable.

"You have four small children in the house" the doctor had said. "God forbid what would happen if one of your sons was injured and started bleeding. The leopard could taste the blood and attack the children. Your Raja is a fully-grown leopard. You have to get rid of him! He belongs in the jungle, not in the house."

My dad knew he was right. But I hated the doctor. I broke down in tears.

"But Raja is not a wild animal!" I said. "He is part of our family. Look Dad, I'm hugging him! He is always fed cooked food in our home. Please Dad, I beg you! Don't send Raja away to the jungle, he is my brother. He cannot defend for himself there. The other wild animals will kill him!"

I was determined not to let Raja be sent to the jungle, but my dad was not prepared to listen, however much I sobbed and howled. Raja was taken away and released in the jungle. I was very sad and very worried about how he would survive. I did not even feel like eating. I knew Raja would not be eating, so why should I?

A few days later I asked Dad to take me to the jungle to see how Raja was doing, but he would not. It took me a long time to get over losing Raja.

The Second World War was now over and many soldiers were being discharged from the army. My stepbrother Bachu came home; he had been trained in the army as a motor mechanic. I was too young to remember Bachu's homecoming, but my mother told me he was wearing his army uniform and was tall and handsome. Everyone was very happy to see him living with us again.

My mother got along very well with Bachu, but my father always had problems and arguments with him. They were working very hard together to make a go of the transport company. Somehow they seemed to have all the bad luck, as the truck always had mechanical problems. It was old and needed continuous maintenance. Dad was spending a lot of time and money on it and did not have enough money to buy a new one.

The problem with the truck created many disputes between father and son. Money was tight in the home and we were just about managing to live from day to day. This led to further arguments. In the end Bachu decided to leave home, and went off to Tanganyika. We four brothers and my mum were all very sorry to see Bachu leave. My mum tried very hard to persuade him not to go. We felt helpless and kept on crying. My father was very stubborn and too proud to ask Bachu not to go, so he went off to his friend's house while all this was going on.

After Bachu left, my father gave up his business altogether, and never started another. He started drinking too much. Bachu did not contact us boys after he left home, though he did get in touch with my mum. He told her he was sorry to leave home, but he was never coming back. Mum tried her best to persuade him to come back home, but Bachu was adamant.

After a while our contact with Bachu was completely lost. Then a few years later a neighbour in Jinja contacted my parents to tell them that Bachu was dead. He had been murdered two days before. He apologised for making us wait for this sad news, but in those days communication was very poor.

Bachu had been working for them in a town called Mwanza, in Tanganyika. No-one ever found out why he had been killed. My mum asked my dad to go to Tanganyika to see what had happened, but he preferred to stay and drown his sorrows in alcohol.

My mum used to have a sewing machine, and to bring in a little money she learned to stitch dresses and do alterations for people she knew. She also used to darn clothes for the children of a wealthy family, who were about my age. They felt sorry for us and gave us clothes their children didn't need any more, so I had them to wear.

One day I was with some friends when the boy from the rich family came to me and said sarcastically how nice his clothes looked on me. Fortunately no one heard him, or it would have been very embarrassing for me. I felt very bad and helpless and asked myself why I had to go through all this. I wanted to tell my mum about this incident, but I knew she could do nothing about it and would only be hurt if I told her.

I was now 10 years old and very aware of how little money we had. I had had to become an adult at a very early age because of the hardship we lived in. I always used to help my mum to do the housework and deliver clothes to her customers.

One day Poppy the dog became ill, and Mum tried to give him some sort of medicine. After losing Raja it was too much for me. I was very much attached to Poppy. I knew he was very ill and was suffering and I hoped his death would be quick, but at the same time I was praying for him to get well soon. But he was going from bad to worse, and a few days later he died. I sat in a corner and cried, and my mum took me in her arms and helped me to calm down. Then she told me to take Poppy and bury him somewhere away from our home. I had a bicycle with a carrier, so I tied Poppy to it, along with a spade, and rode to the sports ground. I was careful to go late in the afternoon so that no-one would be there to see what I was up to.

Twice as I was riding to the sports ground, Poppy fell from the bike and I had to tie him back on again. When I got there I made sure no-one was looking, dug a hole in the ground as fast as I could and quickly buried the dog. Then I jumped on my bike to ride away as quickly as possible before anybody could see me. But as I got on to my bike, I turned for a last look and saw the tip of Poppy's tail sticking out of the ground. I decided to forget about it and ride away.

When I got home my mum asked me if it had gone OK.

"Everything's fine Mum, don't worry," I said.

"Why do I see guilt on your face then? What happened?" I told her I had buried Poppy OK, but I had left his tail sticking out of the ground.

Because of our poverty, the Government granted me a free education. I was born very strong-headed and felt it was beyond me to accept such charity, but I had no choice, so I reluctantly swallowed my pride and accepted. I joined a class of 30 students.

One day when I was 16 years old, an inspector from the Ministry of Education came to our classroom. "Any free students please stand up," he said.

I looked around my class, hoping there were other free students like me so I wouldn't feel too bad about it. But I was the only one. I reluctantly stood up, as I had no alternative. All the other students were looking at me, and I was greatly embarrassed, as I had never told anybody, including my friends, about my free education. My pride was very badly hurt. I decided to leave the school and go somewhere away from Jinja.

I told my teacher I was leaving the school. He did not want me to go. He asked me not to leave over such a small matter, as he could see a good future for me. But I was not prepared to continue in a school where all the students knew I was living on charity.

I was devastated. I wanted to go home to my mother for comfort. I wanted to ask her why we were cursed with such poverty, but I suppressed my feelings. I did not want to tell my mum, because she would be so hurt.

The headmaster called me and asked me not to leave the school. He said I was a bright student and that in future I might perhaps get a scholarship to go and study in UK. I told him the inspector should not have made such an announcement in front of everybody. He should have called the free student to the office to discuss the matter privately. The head said it would not happen again, but for me the damage had been done. I could not tolerate facing my friends and the other students. So after six years' study, I left.

My older brother Shashi and his family were now living in the town of Entebbe, south west of Kampala. It was a beautiful little town which looked as if it had been built in a huge, beautiful garden. In those days it was the capital of Uganda and had an international airport.

When I arrived in Entebbe I went to stay with my brother Shashi, hoping he would find me some work. Shashi was working in the Public Works Department, or the Ministry of Works. I didn't have much education, but I was able to get a job at the PWD. At the same time I was determined that one day I would be someone important. I never wanted to go though poverty again.

I worked at the PWD in Entebbe for two years and gained a lot of experience. I also learned the English language properly, by listening to people. When I made mistakes, they would correct me. In this way I gained the confidence to enable me to move forward in life.

After a while I realised that the job at the PWD was not for me and started looking for a better opportunity. The population of Uganda was small, only about six million people, so opportunities were scarce.

I decided to look for a job with an airline. I wanted to see the world.

CHAPTER THREE

CLEARED FOR TAKE-OFF

I was told there were two vacant positions with East African Airways at Entebbe airport. One was a job as a traffic clerk, checking in passengers. The other was in the cargo office, working shifts. I decided to apply to be a traffic clerk.

It was very hot day when I arrived at the office of East African Airways, and there was a long queue of people applying for jobs. I was afraid of being rejected, so I was tempted to give up and not to bother applying, but I decided that I should go ahead.

After a while I was called in to be interviewed. I was very nervous, as I always had a complex about my poor education. I was hoping the questions wouldn't be too difficult. The manager taking my interview was in his airline uniform, but he had a very relaxed attitude. He asked me some simple questions; I can still remember them clearly. He asked what BOAC stood for, and I said British Overseas Airways Corporation. On his table there was an electric fan going full speed. The manager asked me how many blades it had. I went to the fan, switched it off and told him it had four blades. He laughed and said he could not offer me the job as a traffic clerk, as it had already been given to a girl, but he could offer me a job in their cargo office.

So in 1959 I started my new career with East African Airways. It was an exciting moment to start working for the airline and wearing the uniform.

East African Airways belonged to the three countries of East Africa – Kenya, Uganda and Tanganyika. I was appointed as a junior cargo officer working shifts, which meant 24 hours on, 48 hours off. Slowly I got used to working late nights and weekends. When my training and probation period was over I was promoted to Duty Cargo Officer. After a year I was promoted to Senior Cargo Officer. All the working staff were very co-operative and we were always prepared to share work with each other.

The head office was in Nairobi. There were some other airlines operating through these countries, including BOAC, SAS and Sabena (the former Belgian national airline), and East African Airways was the handling agent for them. The airport was small but very busy. We had the satisfaction of getting the work done and seeing the turn-round met each time for every flight.

Working in the EAA cargo department, there was always some cargo lifting involved in my work. A year after I started I began to feel pain in my stomach. The doctor told me I was suffering from a hernia and would need an operation. He booked me into the Nakasero hospital at Kampala. After the operation I had to stay in the hospital for a few days to recover.

During my stay I met a patient who had a plaster on his leg. When I asked him what had happened to him, he said he had been in a car accident very far away from Kampala, in the middle of nowhere. Nakasero was the only hospital which could take care of such a problem. There was no ambulance service available in the village where it had happened and the villagers had to somehow get him to Kampala very quickly, as he was screaming with pain. They had decided to put a mattress in the back of a small truck and drive him there. To numb the pain, they made him drink a lot of whisky. It worked, but he was drunk for two days.

The shifts of 24 hours on, 48 hours off gave me lots of free time, so I decided to become a member of the sports club in Entebbe. I started playing cricket again, and table tennis. I was enjoying the table tennis particularly and had a good grip on the game. We use to arrange tournaments. I thoroughly enjoyed them and sometimes used to win.

I was sharing an apartment on the third floor with no lift, with a friend who was also working for East African Airways. The apartment had one bedroom with two beds, one small sitting room, kitchen and a bathroom. EAA had a six-seater Volkswagen van to take staff to the airport and bring them home again.

One day someone gave me two small kittens. I was an animal lover, so I enjoyed playing with them. A week later, I was given three more kittens. After a while they started multiplying, and eventually I had 26 cats.

At that time you could not buy tinned cat or dog food in Africa, so my cook had to prepare food for all these cats. He used to complain that he had to cook more food for the cats than for me and my room-mate. Sometimes the cook would get fed up and resign. It was a hard job to have to keep on finding a new cook.

I had were eight favourite cats who used to sleep with me, and during the night others would join them. They would purr like little motorbikes. I use to snore too, so the noise was very loud. My room-mate said I was crazy to have so many cats. He complained that some of them were getting into his bed too, and if he pushed them away they would scratch him. He said that if I didn't do something about it he would have to find somewhere else to live. There was only one thing to do. I told my room-mate to go and find another place to live.

The cats learned to recognise the sound of the Volkswagen's engine, and as soon as they heard it they would come rushing down the stairs to greet me. The landlord was staying on the second floor with his family, and one of them would frequently get caught in the middle of the rush of cats charging down the stairs. The landlord said this was dangerous as someone might fall and be injured. He told me to get rid of the cats or find somewhere else to live.

Now I had to find a new home for my cats. I had an Italian friend called Dino who also liked to collect cats. He had 10 of them and was living alone. When I told Dino what had happened he told me to bring the cats to him. He would be happy to have a family of 36 cats. He said he lived in a big house, so there was no problem. I was happy to settle my problem that way, and my cook was even happier.

Our neighbouring country, Belgian Congo, a French-speaking country, won independence on June 30 1960 and was given a new name, Zaire. There were serious political problems in Zaire, long before independence, because of resistance by the native Congolese to colonialism. Now the problem flared up in a very big way. The African nationals in Congo had not been treated well by the Belgians, so they did not want foreigners living there.

The Congolese army could not control the violence, which escalated to an unbelievable magnitude. It was total chaos. There was a lot of killing, and the Belgians and other European and Asian communities started fleeing the country. A few of the Europeans were killed, while others fled to the safe zone of Uganda.

Entebbe airport was a small airport, but because of the growth in the aviation industry there were many new scheduled airlines, and the existing airlines started to operate more flights. We airline staff were already struggling to cope. On the top of this we started getting many flights carrying refugees from Zaire, which made things even worse.

The political problems created an additional dimension. Entebbe became an extremely busy airport. After an appeal to the United Nations, Entebbe became a hub for the UNO and the refugees. We were very busy handling the incoming and outgoing aircraft, and we worked round the clock.

Sometimes I handled incoming flights which were bringing wounded people and children whose parents had been killed in Zaire. We used to feel very sorry for them, but there were doctors and nurses at the airport to help them. The incoming passengers were sent on to their home countries. It took many weeks for Entebbe airport to calm down and return to normality.

After I went back to my regular duties at the airport, the Cargo Manager told me one day that we were expecting a very urgent consignment from Nairobi, a vital engineering component. The new General Manager, a South African, told me to make sure of the safe arrival of this small but very urgent part. I would have to find it quickly when the plane landed, as the transit stop was only one hour.

I searched for the part everywhere, but could not find it. The General Manager was very angry, and told me I was no good and had failed in my duties. He said my daily performance was poor anyway.

Later on we found that the part had been given to a crew member at Nairobi, so that on arrival at Entebbe he could hand it over to me. No-one from Nairobi told me about this, and the crew member forgot to give it me and instead carried it on to London. I explained to the manager what had happened, but he was not prepared to listen. The next day he called me to his office and repeated his complaints. Then three days later he called me in yet again. He was very unpleasant to me and in his South African accent he abused me with a racist remark. I was not prepared to accept his abusive language, and I abused him in return. The manager told me I was fired. But I had already written a letter of resignation, and I took it out of my pocket and handed it to him. That was how my three years with East African Airways ended.

All business in East Africa was booming and there was a serious shortage of experienced staff. Having the experience in the industry, I applied for a job with British United Airways. This was a private airline based at Gatwick Airport, near London, with a sales office in Kampala.

British United Airways offered me a job as Cargo Sales Manager, and gave me a company car. Though my job was based in Kampala, I had to travel to Entebbe three times a week to look after flights at the airport. In this way I was doing two jobs - marketing passenger and cargo services in Uganda and attending flights as an operations manager at Entebbe Airport. The BUA flights were operating between Gatwick, Salisbury in Rhodesia (now Harare) and Nairobi, all passing though Entebbe. I had to work very hard to keep up with my two jobs.

In addition to all these duties I sometimes had to travel as airline crew to Salisbury and Nairobi, if the station manager was on leave. I would stay in a hotel in Salisbury and come back the next day to Entebbe. On the day I travelled for the first time as the airline crew member from Entebbe to Salisbury, there were eight other crew members on the same flight. I was responsible for making my own hotel booking in Salisbury.

When I arrived at the hotel with the other crew, the reception clerk told me they did not have a room for me. I said that was not possible, and showed him the copy of the telex confirmation. The receptionist told me that they could book me into another hotel, in the Indian area of Salisbury.

I knew what this was about – we all knew about the apartheid in Rhodesia. I refused to leave, so the manager came to see me. He insisted that I had to go to another hotel. But the rest of the crew were listening to all this. The captain said that if the hotel would not accommodate me, they would cancel the airline's contract with the hotel. The hotel manager gave me a room.

The manager then came to my room to tell me that I must stay in my room and they would serve all my meals to me there. I refused to accept such a condition. I was very angry with the manager, and told him to get out of my room.

When we all met up in the bar for a drink before going in to dinner, it was a most difficult time for me. All the whites were staring at me as if I was an animal in a zoo. The rest of my colleagues tried to make it easier for me by treating me as part of the crew.

When we entered the restaurant all the white Rhodesians stared at me with anger in their eyes. I was keeping a brave face, but I was angry too. I was also nervous and very uncomfortable. One of our airhostesses noticed my discomfort and held my hand as we entered the restaurant, which was comforting to me.

After this incident it got a little better, and I continued going to the same hotel whenever I was in Salisbury, though the white staff working at the hotel did not like me.

Meanwhile business started to get better and better, both with the passenger and the cargo business. My duties involved travelling to all the game parks in Uganda and giving airline brochures and posters to them to be displayed at the game lodges. The lodges were a long way from Kampala, so I would stay at the game park hotel overnight and go back to Kampala the next day.

One day I arrived at the game park hotel where I was booked in to be told that the hotel was fully booked and they could not offer me a room. It was a genuine mistake. I had no choice but to travel to another game park hotel. It was a long journey, and I was driving fast to avoid arriving late.

As I drove through the darkness I lost my way. Then I realised that the engine of my car was overheating. The engine started making a whistling noise. I was afraid to get out of the car in the middle of a game park, so I decided to keep on driving slowly and follow the telegraph poles, hoping they would lead me to a village. I was hungry and very thirsty, but I had no food or water with me.

Suddenly in the headlights I saw a leopard ahead, and it certainly wasn't my Raja. It was huge. It strode majestically towards the car. This was my scariest moment of the life. I knew the strength of a leopard and knew it could easily climb over the bonnet of my car and break the windscreen. I was frozen with fear.

Fortunately, just then something moved in the grass at the side of the road, and the leopard ran towards it. I breathed a sigh of relief, but I was still very scared in case the leopard decided to come back for me.

I did not see the leopard again. I kept on driving until I saw the dim lights of a village. It did not seem to have electricity, but there were portable kerosene lights.

I stopped the car, and someone came out of one of the huts and walked towards me. He could not speak English, but he could speak Swahili, and fortunately not the tribal language, which I would have had difficulty with.

"Jambo bwana!" he said (hello sir).

"Jambo, habari yako?" I replied (hello, how are you). "Mimi na choka sana ebu, sayidia mimi" (I am very tired, please help me). I told him about the problem with my car and said it seemed to be a leak from the radiator. We checked and found the cap was loose.

"You must have been travelling for a long time," he said. He offered me tea and some matoke (raw banana, boiled and mashed) with peanut sauce, which I very much appreciated, as I was very hungry. Then he helped me to fill the water tank of my car. I was very grateful to him

"Asente sana" I said (Thank you very much). He pointed towards the direction of the hotel I was heading for

"Endelya moja pu moja" he said (keep on going straight). The hotel was only half an hour away. I arrived very late and went straight to sleep. The next day I was back in Kampala, and very happy to be back in civilisation.

We used to have many tourists coming to East Africa, mainly from Europe and a few from the USA. Kenya, Uganda and Tanganyika all had a lot to offer. The game parks had five-star hotels which offered very good accommodation, food and drinks. They operated safari tours which took tourists to see the animals, and most of the tourists were interested in seeing all the three countries.

We airline staff used to have fun watching tourists coming down the aircraft stairs, as many of them were already dressed in their khaki shorts. They often looked ridiculous. Their shorts were too long to be shorts and too short to be trousers. They wore safari jackets with lots of pockets, khaki hats and boots and had cameras, and binoculars hanging on their shoulders.

Their knowledge of East Africa was very poor. Some of them seemed to imagine they were arriving straight into the jungle. The Americans in particular would ask us if they would be seeing wild animals in the area round the airport. Sometimes we would see them holding up their binoculars or telescopes and looking for animals as they walked up to the airport building.

We airline staff used to joke that these people were looking for Tarzan and Jane. We would tell them, sir, the game park is a long way from here, you will be going there tomorrow by car. By car? They would say, surprised. Yes, by car, not on the back of an elephant!

There was a five-star hotel in Entebbe, the Lake Victoria Hotel. All the tourists used to come and stay there for three or four days before going on to the game parks. Most of them would then stay about three days in the park. The tourists were fascinated to go on safari escorted by the game warden and see the animals and the landscape. After they had completed the safaris in Uganda they would come back to Entebbe and take an East African Airways flight to Nairobi or Dar es Salaam to see the game parks there. Tourism was big business for all the three countries of East Africa. They all had their individual attractions.

One day I took a ride in a small coach from the Lake Victoria Hotel to Kampala. There were some American tourists travelling in the same coach. We were passing through the streets of Kampala when one of them pointed at a Kibuli mosque

"Young man, is that the Taj Mahal?" he said.

"No sir, it is a mosque. The Taj Mahal is in India, not in Africa."

The tourist did not believe me. "I have seen a picture of the Taj Mahal and it looks just like this building," he said. Fortunately one of the other tourists backed me up and told him that no, this was not the Taj Mahal.

It would not be longer before I would have bigger problems to think about than the ignorance of tourists.

CHAPTER FOUR

TROUBLE IN THE AIR

Now that East Africa was flourishing, thanks to the booming economy, the African politicians were putting pressure on the British Government to give them independence. The three countries were increasingly working and trading with each other.

The Government decided to give them their independence one at a time. Tanganyika was granted independence on December 9 1961, and became Tanzania. Uganda became independent on October 9 1962 and Kenya on December 12 1963.

After winning independence, the countries all decided to create their own currencies to replace the East African shilling. Uganda had the Ugandan shilling, Kenya the Kenyan shilling and Tanzania the Tanzanian shilling. The value of their shillings remained the same, 20 to £1 sterling.

Most of the Indians living in East Africa had British passports, while some continued to hold Indian passports. Other nationalities, such as the British, Greeks and Italians, had their own national passports. All had residence permits allowing them to stay in their respective countries. Our way of life was unchanged, and businesses continued as they had during the years of British rule. We could see all three countries thriving and growing fast.

Now that the doors were open to the rest of the world, we were beginning to see more people coming from Germany, France, Italy, India and China to trade with these countries. They opened businesses in collaboration with African and Indian companies. It was a great opportunity for all countries, including the host countries, and brought success to all. Life in Uganda was changing for the better. The shops had more choices, selling goods from different countries. The infrastructure of the roads and footpaths was being improved.

The countries all had their own strengths and assets. Kenya was always very strong in agriculture and dairy produce. Uganda had a copper mine, along with tea, coffee and sugar plantations. Tanzania had a number of mineral resources, including gold and diamonds. The trading between the countries promised to build stronger economies for all three.

The Asian communities, mainly Indians, were running businesses large and small. In fact the entire economy had been developed by the Asians, while the administrations of the countries were run by the British communities. We did not yet realise that as time went on the success of the immigrant communities would prove their downfall, and the downfall of Uganda itself.

Milton Obote, the first elected prime minister of Uganda, praised the Indian community, saying we were its backbone. He recognised that Uganda's prosperity was down to us. However he was not happy to leave the Indians in control of the success and wealth they had created, and he started pushing for Africanisation. He wanted the African people not just to share in the Indian-owned businesses but also to control them. He wanted them to be given 51 per cent of shares in the businesses, as well as taking over key positions from the British civil servants. He thought this was the best way to control the country for a better life for Africans.

The news media backed him up by starting to criticise the Indian community in Uganda. The Africans very much resented the fact that the Indians were effectively controlling the economy. The government started refusing to extend work permits for expatriates. The trading licences of many Asian shops were cancelled, or not renewed. The Indian community started feeling rejected and outcast. We Indians felt that it was quite unfair to force the issue of Africanisation, instead of simply giving Africans the chance to compete. Because of the uncertainties, some of the Asian community started sending their money out of Uganda, and a few of them decided to leave the country altogether.

Meanwhile, as I was doing well with British United Airways, they promoted me to the post of District Passenger and Cargo Manager. I was busy promoting cargo and passenger businesses and travelling all over Uganda, while still attending night flights at Entebbe airport. We took on more people at the airport to cope with the flow of passengers and cargo in and out of Uganda. Since I was doing well Jinny and I decided to get married, and we married in January 1965. Our first son, Sohail was born in November 1965, and our second, Sunil, followed in September 1968.

My younger brother Manu was in southern India, studying to be an aeronautical engineer. After the first year of his studies he came to Kampala for a vacation, and I paid for his education and lodging. When I saw my brother I was shocked to see how much weight he had lost. I asked him why, and he told me the diet in southern India was not suitable for him, but he could not afford the northern Indian food he was used to. He said that in Kerala in South India the local people ate food cooked in coconut oil, and that to live on his low budget he had to eat rice and tamarin juice, which he could not digest.

I felt very bad to hear this, and promised myself that somehow I would send more money to my brother. We Indians who were born in East Africa had very little knowledge of India and the way Indians lived in their homeland. We had developed a different culture, diet and way of life.

Since my promotion as a district passenger and cargo manager, I had stopped going to Entebbe airport at night. The airline appointed a station manager to replace me on night duty. But the continued expansion had created a vacancy in our airline at the airport. I asked my boss to let me continue working at night so I could earn more money to pay for a better diet for my brother. My boss was reluctant to do this, as he said I was already doing too much. I said it would only be for two years as my brother would have graduated by then, and he reluctantly agreed.

Eventually Manu graduated and returned to Uganda. I was very happy to see him back home, but the extra work had given me two years of hell. After my night flights departed at midnight each day I had to drive back 20 miles to Kampala. I would have to stop on the way and pour some water from a bottle on to my face to stop myself going to sleep while driving.

When I had completed six years with British United Airways I was approached by a well-known cargo agent, who offered me a job as General Manager. I knew this company was not doing too well and their manager had been asked to leave very suddenly. It was an IATA air and sea cargo logistics company, exporting and importing cargo all over the world. There were four directors – a director of finance, two accountants and two African silent partners.

They offered me a car and a house to stay in Entebbe, and the salary was more than I was earning at British United Airways. But I was very reluctant to leave BUA, as the company was stable and I was very comfortable in my job and earning good money. I enjoyed working with my colleagues. There was no reason for me to leave my employment.

I declined their offer, but the finance director of the cargo agency would not give up. He was determined to make me their General Manager. After a few meetings I laid down my terms for joining the company. I would promote the business and be given profit targets, and if I met them they would make me their managing director.

The finance director wanted to increase the final target, which was a great challenge. The other directors thought I would not be able to fulfil the terms of the agreement and so would not qualify to become managing director.

I had been working for BUA for six years, and it was very difficult for me to resign. When I told my manager that I was handing in my notice, he was shocked. He offered me more money and a change of car. I told him I wanted to move forward in my life and that I had not only been offered better money but had the chance to become a partner in the new company. The manager tried very hard to persuade me, but I would not change my mind. He was very sorry to lose me.

So in December 1968 I took on my new position as General Manager of this air cargo and shipping logistics company. I had mixed feelings - fear of failing the new challenge, yet confidence that I would succeed.

The house they gave me was in a peaceful spot on a white sandy beach by Lake Victoria at Entebbe. It had previously been a nightclub called Lido. It was a long building facing the lake, with a long veranda, and the roof was supported on wooden poles. The company had converted it to provide a private office, a general office and a small warehouse. Two large wooden sliding gates divided the main office from the servants' quarters. There were two bedrooms and a large sitting-room with a bar. The front of the building faced the lake and a beautiful garden ran down to the beach. There was parking for three cars.

It was the only building on a very long beach, totally isolated and away from the main town. A main road behind the building carried traffic between Entebbe airport and Kampala. The end of the runway almost touched the road.

At night we could hear the waves breaking on the shore. It was a beautiful home and we very much enjoyed it. But we had to think of security at night, so we hired two German Shepherd dogs and two askaris, night watchmen, who guarded us round the clock. A little later we bought a German Shepherd puppy of our own and called her Lindsey.

My father was now living with us in Entebbe. He met some people who were very religious and became very friendly with them. He started visiting a temple every now and again and gave up drinking alcohol altogether.

One day he told me that he wanted to go away to India for a time. I tried to discourage him, reminding him that he was elderly and a diabetic. We had no relations in India, so if anything happened to him it would be very difficult to help him. But he was adamant, as usual. I had no alternative, so I bought him an airline ticket and gave him some money for his trip.

He went to stay in a small village called Kundla in Gujarat, and wrote to me occasionally. One day I received a telegram from a friend of his in Kundla, saying "Your dad is very ill, please come to Kundla urgently." I was very busy with my new job as General Manager, but I had to drop everything and go to India. I flew to Nairobi to catch an Air India flight to Bombay and then a connecting flight to Bhavnagar, the nearest airport to Kundla. I arranged a taxi and told the driver to stay in Kundla until I was ready to return to Bhavnagar, as it would have been difficult to get another taxi.

As we drove through the narrow streets of Kundla many children ran behind the taxi and tried to climb up on to it. I asked the driver why they were behaving this way, and he said it must be because they had never seen a car before.

Finally I arrived at the hospital. I did not like the cramped little ward where my father was sleeping close to other patients. My dad was very pleased to see me. He told me he had met with an accident while getting on the bus. His leg was injured, and because he was diabetic it had gone septic. I told the doctor that I was not happy with the state of the hospital and would like to move my father to a better hospital in the nearby city of Rajkot.

The doctor asked how I was going to move him, and I said in an ambulance. He laughed and said there was no ambulance available in this area, and in any case it was better for him to stay where he was.

"I must tell you that your father's condition is very critical," he said. "I can't help him as I don't have suitable medicine for him." He blamed the system for this. I was angry and felt helpless, cursing the 'system' for the lack of a decent hospital and proper medicine. I sent a telegram to my brother Shashi in Kampala and asked him to come to Kundla immediately.

Next day I left for Bhavnagar and flew back to Uganda. A couple of days later I had a telegram from Shashi saying our father had died just before he had arrived in Kundla.

It was 1969, and I threw myself into my work. A cargo agent's responsibility is to generate cargo for the airline and the shipping line and earn commission from the carrier; it is harder than working for an airline. I started working to win back our old customers and look for new ones. We were mainly exporting fresh fruit and vegetables by air to Europe, but not in large quantities as in Kenya. We were also exporting tea and coffee by sea to Europe. We were importing more goods than we were exporting, as Uganda did not have manufactured goods to sell overseas.

Uganda was a small market, so I decided to be innovative and create new cargo markets for the airlines. I approached some farmers who were not making enough money from their traditional crops. I had a source of seeds for capsicum, courgettes and other vegetables which could be exported to Europe, so I met some farmers and encouraged the farmers to grow these seeds. It would provide a better income than their conventional crops. I told them that if they would grow produce from my seeds there would be buyers for it in Europe, and said I would give them the contacts of the European importers so that they could communicate directly with them. I promised to help them if they had any difficulties.

Uganda being a very fertile land, some of the farmers started growing these vegetables successfully and exporting them to the contacts I supplied. The return was good, and soon other farmers followed. Soon vegetables were being exported to Europe in large quantities. Neither I nor my company wanted to share the farmers' profit; our interest was in expanding the air freight business from Uganda, because our profit would come in commission from the airlines. This was a small project, but it was this kind of initiative that created jobs and prosperity, not only for the farmers but also for the whole country. The farmers were happy with the money they were making. The word spread among the farming community and new farmers were soon sharing in the growth.

Our company started doing well with all this new business, while our existing customers were expanding. As a result we met all our targets within eight months of my joining the company, and I was duly promoted to Managing Director. The expansion continued, and we employed more staff in both the Entebbe and Kampala offices.

We also started exporting various animals by air to Europe. One of our customers, a German, was a professional animal trapper. He was mostly supplying zoos, but he also sent monkeys to Europe for experimental purposes.

One day the trapper was delayed. He turned up late at the airport, with three plywood boxes with holes drilled into them so that the animals could breathe. I was annoyed, as the trapper was late and the wooden boxes did not look very secure. One contained some brightly-coloured tropical birds, one a python and the other a large and very lively crocodile.

I told the customer that the boxes containing the crocodile and the python were not packed to my satisfaction, as there were not enough nails securing them. I told him I could not allow the consignment to go. He pleaded with me, saying his customers were waiting in Denmark for the animals. He said he had a hammer and nails with him and would sit in the back of the truck and nail the boxes properly during the drive to the airport.

"Sam, you worry too much" he said. "It looks OK to me. Don't worry, everything will be all right."

It was an SAS (Scandinavian Airline System) flight to Copenhagen via Athens. The flight landed on time at Entebbe and we had very little time to load the aircraft. I had little choice but to trust my customer, but when the job was done I felt extremely stressed.

We loaded the aircraft and it took off on time, but I was full of doubt. My customer had an odd expression on his face, and I was suspicious. I asked him if he was sure he had done the packing properly, and again he told me not to worry, but I did not trust his smile.

My instincts were proved disastrously correct. Next morning I had a call from the manager at SAS, who read me a telex. It said that when our flight had arrived at Athens airport, the cargo staff had opened the aircraft door to find themselves staring straight into the gaping jaws of the crocodile. They quickly slammed the door and abandoned all attempts to unload the plane. The baggage and the cargo for Athens had to be left on board, as no-one there was qualified to handle such a situation.

The manager at Athens alerted the manager at Copenhagen, and they called in specialist staff to handle the problem. They found the crocodile loose in the aircraft hold, and managed to capture it. The python was loose too, and had some feathers of the birds in the mouth. The birdcage was empty.

I was laughing as I visualised the scene, but the airline manager did not think it was funny. He said he was sending me a claim. I called my customer to tell him what had happened and say how angry I was with him for not securing his animals properly.

"Sam, you know those birds were very valuable" he said. "Can you imagine the financial loss to me?" I was furious at this response and banged the receiver down.

There was political rivalry between the politicians of Uganda and Kenya in various trading lines. Uganda did not like Kenya to have the upper hand. They wanted to slowly separate their trading lines and become an independent source of agricultural and dairy products.

One fine morning I was reading the national newspaper, Uganda Argus. The headline said Uganda was going to start importing bulls and Jersey cows by air from the UK for Uganda Meat Packers. The airline charters were organised by the Uganda Development Corporation (UDC), a government subsidiary, who also paid for the return flights. It was a great opportunity for my company to get this business, as there were going to be 26 flights from the UK to Entebbe with cattle over a two-month period. They would be returning empty to the UK, so there was an opportunity to send cargo on the return leg.

I did not know the boss of UDC, so I contacted my African partner and asked him to introduce me to the CEO so that I could try to win this contract. We went together to the UDC office.

I then had an idea. UDC was exporting a lot of tea by sea to UK, so we could use the return flights to send it by air instead, to everyone's benefit. I presented my project to the boss of UDC and told him we could save him money by putting cargo on the return flight. UDC would benefit from the charges and we would get the usual five per cent commission. I explained that they would pay no more than the sea freight charges for flying the tea to the UK, and he agreed it was a sensible project.

I pointed out that the cattle were flying chained to the floor of the aircraft, which would make it very dirty. Our company would handle the aircraft instead of East African Airways, and we would be able to handle it more efficiently as I had past experience of the airline. We would charge the same handling fees as those of East African Airways.

We got the full contract, though there was a risk in handling the flight without the right ground equipment, such as aircraft stairs and a ground power unit (without GPU you cannot start the aircraft). We had a very short time to put this right. I approached the manager of EAA and asked him if they would lend us their equipment, but he said they would not co-operate with us as they had not got the contract. I then contacted Sabena and asked to hire their equipment. They agreed, and I took on extra staff to handle the flights. Four of them were experienced, while the rest were trainees.

When the first flight came in to Entebbe airport with the cattle, the aircraft was very dirty with cowdung. We were ready with our aircraft handling crew, though I was very nervous as this was the first time I had handled such a difficult and complicated project. Uganda Meat Packers had arranged for a transport company to transport the cattle to the designated farm. The manager of the company was very cooperative and helped me to offload the cattle from the aircraft. Two men had come with the animals from the UK to make sure they arrived safely, and they were a great help.

The offloading was tricky, as we had to use a hydraulic loader which could be raised to aircraft floor level. We slowly lowered the loader with the cattle to the ground, and then with the help of the UMP staff we loaded them on to the truck for transportation to their destination.

Press reporters were there with their photographers taking pictures, and top officials from the government and the UDC were on hand to see the offloading of the cattle. EAA staff also came to see if we could do our job properly.

Everything went well. The next project was to make sure the aircraft was cleaned thoroughly, as we were going to be carrying tea. Any smell would be fatal, because if the tea picked up the smell no-one would buy it. We had 12 hours to clean the aircraft thoroughly, and we did a splendid job.

The outgoing flight left on schedule the next day. After two days a UDC official told me that it had arrived very fresh because it had travelled by air, so the UDC tea department got more money for it. I jumped at this good news and asked to increase our handling charges a little, and this was agreed. The government and UDC officials were very happy to see our operation go off so smoothly. The project became the talk of the town for a long time, and it was all helping Uganda to succeed in cattle farming.

One day we were offloading the cattle when somehow a bull escaped from the loader and ran along the runway. We staff were all running after it when it suddenly stopped, turned towards us and charged. We had to run for our lives. The EAA staff enjoyed watching the little drama as eventually the bull was brought under control. Thank God no aircraft were using the runway at the time.

Shortly after this operation the Ugandan government decided to start its own cargo airline, Uganda Airline. Once again UDC was appointed as the organiser. Because we had handled their charter flights so successfully, UDC asked us to handle the new airline at Entebbe. This was yet another big challenge, but we accepted the contract very happily. Our company was now the biggest cargo logistics company in Uganda.

Now that I had the full backing of the Ugandan government, I told them we urgently needed our own bonded warehouse within the airport to accommodate our cargo, because EAA would not co-operate with us. The government gave us immediate approval, and we were given the money to build the warehouse we needed.

Trans Meridian Airline was appointed to operate as Uganda Airlines, and I flew to the UK to make the necessary arrangements. Our government wanted to fly the Ugandan flag, for political reasons. I wanted to turn this into a huge commercial project, and the government gave me a free hand to move ahead as quickly as possible. We decided to operate one flight per week between Entebbe and Stansted airport.

We hired more office space at Entebbe and took on more staff to start the new venture. We began by diverting our existing customers' cargo on to

Uganda Airlines, but the aircraft was a Canadair CL44 with a huge capacity, so it was difficult to find enough cargo to fill it. We were hiring the ground equipment at Entebbe from Sabena on a contract basis.

We started competing with EAA and other airlines for cargo, and the volume, both import and export, quickly increased. The new business was a great success and it wasn't long before we were operating two flights a week. My personal aim was to get this up to at least four.

Knowing that our neighbouring countries, Rwanda and Burundi, did not have their own airlines, I decided to pay a visit to both countries to meet the government officials and get their approval for landing rights. Burundi had very little interest, but Rwanda was very interested in exporting fresh vegetables and fruit to Europe. We soon had an agreement signed with the government officials in Kigali, the capital of Rwanda.

The fruit and vegetable farmers were enthusiastic, but there was not yet enough cargo to make it commercially viable. Thinking of my previous experience, I gave them contacts for the suppliers of the seeds and the names of importers. The new route to start with was Stansted-Entebbe-Kigali-Entebbe-Stansted.

I could not speak French, the official language of Rwanda, but we could communicate in Swahili. The plan was that I would fly to Kigali from Entebbe each week, before the arrival of the Uganda Airlines flight, to make sure the export cargo was ready. I would then return to Entebbe on the same flight.

At last I received confirmation from Kigali that they were ready to export their product, and made the arrangements for the first flight. Two days before the flight I flew to Kigali to make sure all was in place before the flight arrived. Communication in those days was by telex and phone, and there were great difficulties as the telephone network system from Uganda could operate only via Belgium.

I was very nervous as I waited at the control tower of Kigali airport, because the flight was delayed. I was surprised to get a phone call from the captain of the aircraft, who was in Lusaka in Zambia. He said there was a fault with the aircraft engine, and by the time the flight arrived at Kigali it would be after 7 pm. Night flights were not allowed at Kigali, so they had had to reschedule their arrival to the next day.

I was annoyed about this, as the exporters could not wait until the next day. The cargo was perishable, and there were no cold storage facilities in Kigali, so it had to be flown the same day. I was under great pressure from the customers and the officials of the Ministry of Agriculture. Fortunately the ministry official was given approval by the minister to make an exemption to the rule so that our flight could land at night. Communication was difficult, so I spoke to the control tower at Kigali and persuaded them to let me speak to the captain. After a lot of persuasion, he agreed to make the night landing.

The flight arrived in Kigali just after midnight. As we prepared to load the aircraft we saw armoured tanks rushing towards our aircraft from both ends of the runway. One tank stood right in front of the aircraft and the other by the tailplane. Army jeeps also surrounded the aircraft.

The Commander of the Rwandese Army marched into the airport building with a troop of fully-armed soldiers. I was with the captain and crew and we wondered what was going on. The Commander spoke to us in French, but none of us could speak French so I replied in Swahili. He accused us of being mercenaries and asked us why we had landed at night. In those days there were mercenaries hired by miners in Zaire, the neighbouring country to Rwanda, who would land in Zaire at night.

They wanted to inspect our cargo in case we were carrying arms. I told the captain it was general merchandise and machinery spares, and we had official approval to come in at night. The captain said he was annoyed with me and would not take me back to Entebbe on his aircraft. I said that if he didn't agree to take me back I could mistranslate his words and tell the Commander he was abusing him. The captain got the message, and withdrew his threat.

They inspected the cargo in the aircraft and all was OK, but the Commander still wanted to know why we had landed at night. I showed him proof that the landing had been authorised by the Minister of Agriculture. He checked and found it was in order. The Ministry of Defence had been told, but no-one had told the Commander. It boiled down to poor communications.

At last we were told we could proceed with our journey. We loaded the cargo, took off and arrived safely at Entebbe.

We obtained permanent landing rights for Uganda Air at Kigali Airport, as long as the flight operated before 7 pm, though in an emergency they would allow us to operate after 7 pm. These new arrangements helped both Uganda Air and the government of Rwanda, though we were monitoring the cargo from Kigali.

In those days Uganda Airlines was operating only as a cargo airline. Passenger traffic could have provided additional revenue for them. East African Airways was operating as a domestic airline to all three countries, Uganda, Kenya and Tanzania, and operating on international routes both for cargo and passengers. To run Uganda Airlines as a profitable organisation was a difficult task, and I was very keen to get into the cargo business with Kenya, Tanzania and Rwanda. Importing goods from Europe was more profitable than exporting fruit and vegetables.

We contacted various importers in Kenya, Tanzania and Rwanda and offered them good rates. Many of them were interested. We arranged to help our European suppliers by transporting the cargo - machinery and machine parts - by road to Stansted airport and then flying it to Entebbe to be carried on to Uganda, Kenya, Tanzania and Rwanda. We kept the cargo in transit at Entebbe and despatched it to its final destination on the scheduled airlines. This method was highly successful, and made Entebbe airport the hub of air cargo in East Africa.

As our business was growing, I decided one day to drive to Goma, a town in Zaire, from Kigali. The customs post at Zaire was notorious for extorting money from people entering the country. The customs officer tried to talk to me in French, but I spoke in Swahili. He welcomed me into Zaire. It all seemed rather too easy, which worried me. I checked in at the only hotel in the town, had a shower and went for a drink in the bar.

The customs officer came to see me at the hotel, and I almost choked on my drink when I saw that he was still wearing his dark glasses, even though it was night time. I knew it was a very bad sign. However I pretended I was pleased to see him and put on a fake smile. He seemed very happy to see me, and said how much he liked cognac. I offered him brandy and we talked away on various unimportant subjects. He was drinking his brandy very fast, and I was paying.

"You are going back to Kigali in two days?" he said.

"Yes."

"I have many children. I need money for their milk."

"But I have already spent a lot of money this evening. I don't have any more money with me."

"Then I don't know how you're going to cross the border back into Rwanda."

He was threatening me, and I felt very worried. I told him I could arrange to have some funds tomorrow. He was happy with that and shook my hand, assuring me nothing would happen to me as long as I gave him some money. The next day I saw him before crossing the Zaire frontier and paid him again.

I surveyed the market offered by Goma, and decided that it was a waste of time. But at least I returned to Kigali unharmed, and flew back to Entebbe.

CHAPTER FIVE

THE GATHERING STORM

Back home in Uganda there was growing concern among the Asian community over the new government policy of Africanisation. In the media the Asian community was accused of being a liability to the country. They were saying that the native Africans had to benefit from the prosperity, because Uganda was their country.

All foreigners, including Indians, had a deep-rooted fear and uncertainty about the future. When people talked politics among themselves, they always looked over their shoulders to make sure no-one was listening.

Trading licences were being revoked, and this began to have a serious effect on the Asian community. Some Asian businessmen left Uganda. Others were confused by the situation and were struggling to find a way around it.

While I was working at Entebbe I sometimes saw the Prime Minister, Milton Obote, travelling through with his Ministers. I would also see Idi Amin, the Commander of the Ugandan Army, and his senior officers. There were rumours about a power game between Obote and Amin. Amin was from the Kakwa tribe, perhaps the smallest tribe in Uganda, but he cleverly recruited soldiers from other friendly tribes to strengthen his position. Relations between Amin and Obote deteriorated and eventually Obote demoted him from commander of the armed forces and left him as commander of the army alone.

For Amin, that was the final straw. In January 1971, Obote went to Singapore to attend a Commonwealth conference. One evening while he was away we heard gunshots. Quickly a rumour spread that there had been a coup and the army had taken over the civilian government. At first we could not believe this, as Uganda was the most peaceful and stable country. But it was true. On January 25 Idi Amin took over the civilian government and Milton Obote was deposed. Radio Uganda and Uganda Television announced that Commander Idi Amin was now the Major General and Commander of the Ugandan Army, and hence in charge of Uganda.

Many people were killed in the army quarters, particularly men from the Acholi, Lango and Luo tribes which were loyal to Obote. The slaughter did not stop there - Amin's soldiers went on a witch-hunt. They killed politicians and ministers all over Uganda. Many African nationals were very happy about the coup, and celebrated by dancing and singing on the streets of Kampala. Amin gained popularity not only in Uganda but in other neighbouring African countries, and even became popular internationally.

There was no opposition in the news media to the coup, even though Idi Amin was a self-appointed general and a self-appointed president. Some people in the Asian community were happy about it too, as they were expecting him to reverse Obote's policy of Africanisation. On the other hand, most people in Uganda feared the unknown. The arrival of a military government was creating great uncertainty within the Asian business community, although Amin was encouraging everyone to stay in Uganda and saying the country would be safe for all. He said Uganda needed Indians as they were important for the economy, so we should not worry.

We were living very peacefully in our lovely, isolated home on the beach at Entebbe. I had a company car, plus my own car MG sports car and a speedboat. But after the coup, things began to change. A curfew was imposed – we were not allowed to be out of our homes between midnight and 6 am. We used to hear that soldiers were being murdered all over Uganda, because Amin wanted to get rid of any soldiers who were loyal to Obote. People saw the bodies of dead soldiers in Lake Victoria and the River Nile.

I mentioned that our house was not far from the end of the airport runway. I was told that many soldiers who had supported Obote were being taken to the end of the runway at night to be shot. Our peaceful home became very isolated and the area around it was full of menace. I started to worry about our security. I arranged to have thick wire mesh nailed to the pillars around the residence, which made it like a fortress.

I continued to go to the airport almost every night, coming back home before midnight when our flight had left. Manu was working as an aeronautical engineer there, and sometimes when he was working late he would sleep on a couch in our sitting room. Our second bedroom was occupied by our night nanny, Margaret, and our two children, Sohail and Sunil.

One evening I came home just before midnight and went to sleep around 1am. I was awoken from a deep sleep by a hand shaking my leg

"Amuka!" said a voice. (Get up). I sat up to see a man dressed in a dirty soldier's uniform standing at the foot of our bed pointing his rifle at me. I thought it was a dream, but it was all too real.

"Naa hona nini? Toka qua kitanda!" he said (What are you looking at? Get out of the bed.) He seemed angry.

I stumbled out of bed, very confused, trying to get to grips with what was happening. Jinny lay beside me. I thought she had not woken up, but in fact she was petrified with fear and was pretending to be asleep. To both of us it seemed unreal, a terrible nightmare, but it was all too real. Our house was very isolated, so it was not likely anyone would hear what was going on.

We were terrified that our children might have been harmed. Sunil, our younger son, woke up with the noise, but Margaret quickly gave him a bottle of milk to keep him quite. Sohail still was fast asleep. Margaret came into our room and told us they were all right.

"We are deserters from the Ugandan army," the soldier explained. "We are members of the Acholi tribe, so we are loyal to Mr Obote. Amin's soldiers are looking for us."

Then another soldier came into the room, carrying a machete. The two men started talking to each other in the language of the Acholi, which we did not understand. We had no idea what they were saying, but we were sure it was not good.

There was a full moon, and out of the window I could see three more soldiers. I was very much aware that these men could kill us at any moment.

"Give me your money!" said the soldier. I was very glad to give them some money if it would make them go away, but I was so confused and scared that did not know where to look. Then I remembered that there was some money in a cupboard in the bedroom, so I got out of bed and stumbled over to the cupboard, got out the money and offered it to him.

He threw it back in my face. "There is a safe deposit box in your office" he said. "Open it and give me all the money!"

I told him I did not have the key of the safe-deposit box, it was our cashier who kept it. This was true, but the soldier did not believe me.

"You love your money more than your life!" he said.

"I don't have the key, please believe me!" I pleaded. "If I had the key I would have given you the money by now."

The soldier was angry and asked for the key to my office. I handed it to him, but he was not satisfied. He seized my arm and dragged me with him to the office, leaving the other soldier guarding Jinny. The safe was mounted in the wall. Another soldier joined him and the two of them started trying to break into the safe with the butts of their rifles, but it was too strong.

Now he was even more angry. He pulled me back to the bedroom and told me he was going to kill me. He pulled out two cartridges from his dirty army uniform, pushed them into his gun and thrust the barrel into my chest. I closed my eyes and shivered with fear. I could see my death. Thoughts were flashing through my mind about what would happen to my wife and children when I was dead.

He pulled the trigger. There was a click. "I did not release the safety catch," said the soldier.

By now I was dripping with perspiration from head to toe and thought I was as good as dead. At such a time one dies many times, not just once.

He talked to the soldier with the machete for a while, and again we wondered what they were saying and what they were going to do with us.

"Don't shoot him," the other soldier said. "The noise will wake Amin's soldiers. I had better cut his throat." He held the edge of the machete against my throat.

"Please don't kill my husband!" said Jinny. "My brother-in-law is sleeping in the sitting room, he might have some money." They didn't know about the sitting room.

We all went to the sitting room, where my brother was fast asleep. We woke him and told him the soldiers wanted money and we didn't have enough. We were lucky. He had had his salary that day, and he gave it all to them.

The soldiers looked at me. "Bahati yako mazuri" said the one with the gun (your luck is in your favour). Then they left at last.

We all took a long breath of relief and thanked God for saving our lives. Once they had gone I went to see what had happened to my dogs, my servants and the askaris. They were all locked inside the servants' quarters. They were very happy to see us. We found the soldiers had cut the telephone lines.

The askaris said the soldiers would very probably come back later to try to get more money out of us. We told our servants that we would go to the homes of some friends in the town. The askaris were concerned about the curfew and feared that the real army would catch us breaking the law, but we could not stay there after what had happened. We had no choice other than to drive to our friend's home. We told the askaris they could go home if they wanted to, but they stayed behind, as they knew the soldiers would not ask them for money.

Our ordeal had been going on for three hours by the time we left for our friends' home. Once we got there, we told them all about what had happened. We were still talking when the sun rose the next morning.

When we got back home the next day, our servants told us that the soldiers had indeed returned to see what else they could take. We found they had taken a small transistor radio from our bedroom.

I had to report this incident to the police, but they said such matters were not under their control and I should report the matter to a man called Captain Akiki, who was in charge of security at the airport.

"Don't worry," he said. "We will find these people and punish them."

Our dream home had been the scene of a nightmare, and we knew we could no longer live there. Finding rented property in Entebbe was very difficult, as most houses were purpose-built for their owners. The few rented apartments in the town were all occupied. Most of the houses belonged to the government, as Entebbe was the capital of Uganda.

I had a meeting with my partners, who advised me to stay for now at the Lake Victoria Hotel and try to find a property to rent in Kampala. We decided to stay with our friends rather than in the hotel. We went looking for somewhere to live in Kampala, as well as a school for our children, and found a house in a very good area, Mackenzie Vale in Kololo, a smart suburb of the city. We checked that we had good neighbours around us, as we did not want to live in another isolated house like the one we had left.

We moved to Kololo as soon as we could and found a good school for the children. I now had to drive the 20 miles from Kampala to Entebbe every day, but we had offices in Kampala, so I decided to work from there and get a junior manager to look after the Entebbe office. However I still had to go to Entebbe from time to time.

Life in Uganda was changing rapidly. The soldiers were imposing their own law on the country and democracy started to give way to dictatorship. Many soldiers started abusing their positions, threatening people and extorting money from them.

I set out to win the confidence of Captain Akiki, the man in charge of security at the airport. He was another who liked to wear dark glasses at night. I needed a good relationship with this man, as I knew that otherwise he might create problems for Uganda Airlines by not letting us have landing rights or preventing our staff from working at the airport. He soon became friendly, though I was trying not to get too close to him.

One day he turned up at my Entebbe office with two soldiers, fully armed.

He asked me to give his sister-in-law a job in my office. I told him there was no vacancy, and we had no space for an extra desk anyway.

"Then make some space!" he said.

I asked him if the girl had any experience.

"She has just left school" he said. "You can train her. She can start working with you tomorrow."

I had no choice but to employ this young lady. Our manager interviewed her and found she could speak very little English. I told him to arrange some training with immediate effect.

The young lady was polite and willing to learn, but a few days later she came to the office with bruises on her face. She had been very badly beaten. In the afternoon the captain came to my office. He was very angry about something. He went straight into our general office, pulled his sister-in-law out of the office and started beating her.

"You can discharge her!" he said. "She is no longer working in your office." He took her away. There was nothing I could do about it.

Finally I found a suitably experienced manager, a man who had been my boss at East African Airways and was now retired. I was happy to move to our Kampala office permanently and go to Entebbe airport occasionally.

The leased aircraft we used at Uganda Air was a Canadair CL44. It had a swing tail so that it could be fully opened for loading, and it could also be loaded from the side door. We had quite a few people working for us loading and offloading the aircraft.

One day the aircraft arrived from England loaded with heavy machines, machinery spares and motor vehicle spares to be offloaded. I gave Hassan, the supervisor, instructions to offload the cargo. He was supposed to remove some of the cargo from the tail of the aircraft first and then take the rest from the side, to maintain the balance of the aircraft. We then had to load 25 tons of fruit and vegetables for export back to the UK. I left Hassan to it and returned to my office.

A little while later, Hassan came running to my office in a panic. He said the aircraft was sitting upright like a rocket. I came out of my office and saw the nose of the aircraft pointing up into the air. I had never seen anything like it.

Of course, Hassan had removed the cargo from the side door first and the aircraft, being too tail-heavy, had tilted backwards with its nose high up off the ground. I called the ground engineer and told him he should have been there to look after the safety of the aircraft.

We managed to tie a net in the middle of the aircraft, and started unloading the vegetable and fruit boxes from the side door. We also offloaded the rest of the machinery spares from the tail. Slowly the aircraft tilted back down to its normal position. Fortunately it was undamaged.

CHAPTER SIX

THE SHADOW OF AMIN

Idi Amin, now President and Field Marshal, was always showing off to the media. He drove in a car-racing safari, and of course he won it. He swam for the TV cameras in the pool at the five-star Apollo Hotel in Kampala, and bragged about being the best boxer in the world. All this boasting made him a laughing stock, though no-one laughed to his face.

The mainly Asian and European business community started seeing a rapid decline in business. Uncertainty was growing and everybody was worried about what would happen to the Ugandan economy. The government itself was soon almost bankrupt because of the mismanagement of funds.

The Ugandan government had good diplomatic relations with Israel, which it needed both for trading and military assistance. When the constant increase in air traffic required a new airport terminal at Entebbe, the contract was given to an Israeli company.

During the early months of 1972 Amin made several visits to Israel to ask for military support, money, arms, jet fighters and other military hardware. He wanted all this to wage war on Tanzania, as Obote was living in exile there and Amin saw him as a threat. But Israel understandably would not accept this as a reason for giving military support, and refused. Amin made the same request to Britain, and was given the same answer.

He then visited Libya and other Middle Eastern countries and apparently was offered some limited help. When he came back from Libya he imposed a new rule – he banned women from wearing jeans and short dresses. The newspapers were full of stories about the threat of Uganda declaring war on Tanzania.

In revenge for Israel's refusal to help him, Amin started criticising Israel and praising Hitler. Then he ordered all Israeli nationals working in Uganda to leave within three days. This came as a shocking blow. Many people in Uganda thought Asians and Europeans would be the next target.

The army killings started again, with Amin's soldiers murdering thousands more soldiers in the army barracks. Thousands of soldiers fled Uganda in fear, running away to Tanzania to join Obote. Then the Ugandan army began targeting intelligent and powerful Africans in various government positions, because Amin did not want any competition or threat of any kind to himself.

In September 1972 my own business partner was killed by Amin's soldiers. I still do not know why he was killed. I was shocked and very worried about his family. We all wondered who would be next.

One day I was having a quiet drink on my own in the airport bar when my old 'friend' Captain Akiki came in. It was not a pleasant surprise, but I offered him a drink and we started chatting.

The captain said he had good news – he had been promoted to Commander. I congratulated him.

"You are my friend," he said. "You have helped me in the past and I want to do something for you in return." I did not want to hear what he was going to say next.

"I will turn you into a doome, a real macho man" he said.

"What do you mean?" I said. My voice was shaking.

"You have heard the gunshots at night from the end of the runway?"

"I have heard them."

"Tonight I would like you to come with me in my Jeep to see how we kill our enemies. It is a rare opportunity to see people being killed at close range. It will be the experience of a lifetime for you."

I was very scared. I did not want to see people being killed, but I did not know how to refuse the Captain's invitation. I took a deep breath.

"I respect you and have helped you, but I will not be able to watch these things" I said.

"You are a coward!" he replied.

"I am not a brave soldier like you, I am just a businessman," I protested. "Please forgive me for not taking part in such matters."

The captain laughed. "I was only trying to turn you into a doome" he said.

He drove away in his Jeep, and I took a deep breath and went back to my office.

I had some free time just then, so I started to think about all that was happening. I badly wanted to get away from all these problems. We were living in constant fear of what might happen tomorrow. We were afraid of switching on the TV or opening a newspaper, because we knew there would be more bad news and more politicians condemning Indians and blaming us for all sorts of things. We were afraid of talking to people we did not know, in case they had some connection with the politicians and told them what we had said. We were afraid of looking at the soldiers walking on the streets. Life was full of fear, every step of the way. It was like walking on a tightrope.

I tried to cheer myself up by thinking good thoughts, about what a wonderful life we used to have, hanging out with our friends and family and enjoying the paradise we were living in, going for a spin in the MG or riding in our speedboat on Lake Victoria. But always the fear came creeping back.

Next day as I was working in my office in Kampala, the good dreams of the previous night were shattered. Someone phoned and told me I must watch the TV. We all have to leave Uganda, he said.

It was August 4 1972. Amin announced that he had had a dream in which God had told him that the Asians must leave Uganda. They were doing Uganda no good – he even said we were milking the economy. He had decided that all foreigners not holding Ugandan passports must leave Uganda within three months.

No-one could take in this shocking news, or perhaps no-one wanted to believe it. Many Asians thought it must be a joke. But the news was repeated, and it was clear that the government was taking it seriously.

The Asian community was devastated. There were about 80,000 Asians in Uganda, and very few of them held Ugandan passports. Many had applied for Ugandan citizenship during Obote's administration, but many applications were refused or purposely delayed by the authorities.

Amin said Asians holding British passports were not his responsibility, so the British Government should take them back to Britain. Many Indians did not have passports at all, as they never thought they would need them. These people would become stateless, and we were very concerned about what would happen to them.

On August 6 1971 we held a party at our home to mark my wife's birthday, and many friends were invited. Of course we talked about what we were going to do. None of our friends wanted to leave Uganda. Most of them said Amin would have to reverse the expulsion order, because if he didn't the entire economy would collapse. Uganda would also lose most of its professionals – doctors, lawyers, teachers and other qualified people.

Now that my partner had been so brutally murdered, I had no interest in continuing to live in Uganda. My focus was clear. I knew Amin would not reverse his decision. I told my family to start packing. We did not know what to do with Lindsey, our beautiful dog.

Amin was constantly making TV announcements to say that we in the Asian community must take his threat very seriously. He said he did not want to see any Asians in Uganda after the three-month deadline passed in November.

"You have all been milking the economy of Uganda," he said. "You Asians came to Uganda to build the railways. Now they are running on time, so you can all travel by rail and leave Uganda before the deadline."

He said we would all be sent forms to fill in to give full descriptions of our businesses, properties, houses and offices. From these forms the government would decide which African nationals to give them to. There was no choice in the matter.

He also announced that our private and company bank accounts would be frozen immediately, so our money would not belong to us any more. We would be allowed to withdraw only enough money to enable us to travel out of Uganda. We could take personal belongings of up to 250 kilos per family.

Fortunately I had already withdrawn all my personal money, as I had feared that something like was going to happen. I had given the money to an African friend for safe keeping, until I could tell him where to send it. The Uganda shilling became worthless; it was soon down to about 2500 shillings to a sterling pound.

To our pleasant surprise, we saw advertisements in the Uganda Argus from many embassies, including Canada, Sweden, Austria, Britain and a few other European countries, inviting Asians to go to their country, where they would be given settlement visas. In the UK, settlement visas were mainly restricted to British passport holders. Before this, Asians holding British passport had not been allowed settlement visas for the UK, which had been a source of contention between the British Government and the Asian communities. Britain did not want Asians going to the UK even for holidays, as the government was worried about attracting illegal immigrants.

In my family we all had British passports, so we had the choice of migrating to any European country or Canada. I chose to settle in England, and was able to get visas for our family because of my business connections with UK companies. My brothers Shashi and Manu and their family members were all holding British passports too, so they decided to move to the UK as well. My brother Arvind and his family had already moved to the UK, and my mother had followed them.

There was great confusion after the announcement from Amin saying all Asians must leave Uganda before the deadline. Those holding Ugandan passports were worried as they too had to leave Uganda. Stateless people (those with no passports) and Uganda passport holders of Asian origin were accepted by countries like Europe, Canada, Australia and the USA. Indian and Pakistani passport holders went to their respective countries.

Many prominent business people in Uganda tried very hard to persuade

Idi Amin to change his mind about the expulsion of Asians. He was reluctant to meet anyone from the Asian community, but eventually, he agreed to meet the Asians in the International Conference Hall in Kampala. This was a televised debate and almost everybody was watching. We were all eager to see the outcome, hoping Amin would change his mind. Everyone who was prominent in the business community came to watch this vital conference about the future of our lives.

We had to wait two hours for Amin to arrive. Dressed in his full army uniform, he began his speech with a piece of paper in his hand. He waved it in the air.

"Do you know why I am late?" he said. "I am late because there was a problem with an Indian girl having an African boyfriend. Let me begin with the content of this letter".

He started reading the letter: "There is an Indian girl who is in love with an African boy and they want to get married. The African boy's parents have no objection, but the Indian parents of the girl are objecting to the marriage."

The writing of the letter was in English but in Amin's style. In any case Amin was illiterate and could not have read from the letter. He continued:

"I was called by this girl and I personally went to see her. The girl was in love with the African boy. Her parents were objecting strongly because his family were African. So you can see, you Indians would like to live in Uganda but you don't want integrate with Africans!"

One of the businessmen got up. "Your Excellency" he said. "May I see the letter?" Amin ignored the request and put the letter in his pocket. He went on talking.

"You see, you Asians want to stay in Uganda but you don't like the African people!"

Another businessman got up. "Your excellency, we are asking you to reverse the expulsion order" he said. "You are blaming us for milking the economy of Uganda, but all we have done has been for the progress of Uganda. Our businesses will be ruined, but more importantly the economy of Uganda will completely collapse!"

"We can run the country better than you lot!" said Amin.

Another businessman got up and pointed out that the Asians had built hospitals, schools and universities all over Uganda for the benefit of all people, including Africans. Another said his organisation employed more than 40,000 Africans, and once the Asians left they would all be jobless. But Amin continued running down the Asian communities and saying they had done nothing for Uganda. He was not going to go back on his decision.

Many Asian shops and businesses now started closing down, as there was no point in doing any further business. Most of the other cargo agents' offices soon closed, but I decided to keep our office open to help people who wanted to send their personal belongings overseas. East African Airways was the only company to keep trading.

In happier times I used to see long lines of people outside the cinemas queuing for movie tickets. It used to be my dream that one day we would have so many customers that we would have queues like that. Now my dream came true, but not in the way I had hoped. We had queues of people outside our offices waiting to send their personal belongings, and all our staffs were kept very busy working late hours.

Some people were waiting in the hope that Amin would change his mind, but I was sure he would not. I decided not to take any chances for my family. We packed up our 250 kilos of personal belongings and flew them to London at the first opportunity. I had to stay behind in Uganda to hand over our company to our African partner. It was a tearful farewell at the airport because I could not be sure when I would see my family again, but I was very relieved when they left safely. I kept in constant contact with them after they arrived in England.

Uganda quickly started sliding into chaos. It was like sinking in quicksand. We were constantly told by the local Africans how happy they were that we Asians were leaving. "This is not your country!" they would say. They were all looking forward to taking over our houses, offices and cars for free, thanks to Idi Amin's pronouncement. They would sing and dance in the streets to celebrate our going away.

The army officers were taking people in prominent positions in the African community, such as politicians and senior government officers, seizing them from their offices and houses and putting them in prisons or army barracks. We were very scared of both the army and the local Africans, and hoped matters would not get out of control. It was looking very like civil war, and we were living life in fear from day to day, always wondering if we would still be alive tomorrow.

There was an army prison in Kampala called Makindye prison. We used to call it One-Way Prison, because once people were taken there they never returned home. Most of them were killed. There was a lot of corruption among the soldiers running the prison as they were targeting innocent Indians to extort money. We heard many African prisoners who had been guilty of the wrong politics or belonging to the wrong tribe being taken to Makindye prison.

We were told the soldiers had fun torturing and killing prisoners. They would make them lie face-down in a line on the floor. The first prisoner in the line was given a big hammer and ordered to hit the last prisoner very hard on the head, and then lie down to await his turn to be clubbed to death.

We had an office boy called Samweri who had been working with us a long time. One day he came to me to ask my help to fill in a form. The form was for African nationals wanting to take over a business for free as promised by Amin. I asked him how much he knew about our business.

"Don't worry," he said. "I will learn after I take your business over." I asked my secretary, a Danish national, to help him, as he could not speak English.

We were very busy handling the many people who were sending their personal belongings to their new homes. They would all pay us in Ugandan shillings. They were of course worthless, yet we went on accepting the money and helping people to send their personal effects of 250 kilos per family.

One day as this was going on, one of our staff came to my office and told me an English lady wanted to speak to me. I invited her in. She was quite young and had several bruises on her face and arms. She was in tears. She said she was a teacher from Fortportal, which was a long way from Kampala. She had decided to come to Kampala to take a flight back home to England. She had had to go through three army check blocks.

"They have taken all my money," she said. "I don't know how I will buy my air ticket and send my baggage to England."

I felt so sorry for her that we arranged the airline ticket and sent her baggage to England, all without charge. She said she could send the money from England, but I told her not to worry about the money as we were all in the same boat. We all wanted to get out of Uganda safely.

Late one afternoon an army officer wearing dark glasses and full uniform came to my office and asked if I was Mr Thaker. I was petrified to see the dark glasses, as I knew there was something wrong and I was in trouble.

"Twende!" he said (let's go).

"Where?" I said. "What have I done?"

"You are smuggling the personal effects of your Indian brothers," he said.

"It is not so" I answered. "We are sending people's personal effects to their chosen destinations, as per the new regulations of President Idi Amin."

The Captain removed his dark glasses and looked angrily into my eyes.

"Bahati yako baya!" he said (You will have bad luck). He was determined to take me with him.

"You see that black BMW?" he went on. "That is my car. "I am taking you in the trunk of the car to the famous Makindye prison."

I was frozen with fear, because I knew that if I went to Makindye I would be killed. My secretary reacted quickly, and called my director of finance to come to our office urgently. We had lots of cash in the office, as our customers were all paying cash. We offered the money to the Captain. He took it and put his dark glasses back on

"Taa honana" he said (I will see you again). I told my partner I now had to leave immediately for the UK, as I knew this captain would be back looking for me and demanding more money, and I most certainly did not want to go to Makindye Prison.

My driver drove me home in our company car. When we got there my servants were waiting for me. I had told them over the phone that I would have to leave Uganda that day. They knew what to pack for me.

The servants were all crying and pleading to me not to go. I explained the situation and gave them some money. They were not much interested in money, but they reluctantly accepted it. I told them to go back to their home towns, as they would be safe there.

We had excellent furniture, which would all have to be left behind, but I didn't care about that. I was much more concerned about what would happen to the house after I had left for the UK. I was very worried that the army captain would come looking for me.

I was also very worried about Lindsey, my dog. Somehow she sensed that I was going away. She was very uneasy and kept crying and barking and looking at me with sad eyes. This was a very sad moment for me as Lindsey was part of our family, yet I was not in a position to take Lindsey with me as I had not had time to arrange quarantine.

Lindsey knew my driver George very well, as George would often take him for a ride in the car, which she loved. George loved Lindsey too. In the circumstances I had no choice but to ask George to take Lindsey home. The driver was very happy to take Lindsey, but the dog was refusing to get into the car.

My heart was bleeding at the thought of leaving Lindsey behind. I got into the car, pretending we were just going for a ride, to encourage her to get into the car. But she would not get in, and in the end I had to drag her into it.

I gave some money to George. "Please make sure you look after my Lindsey," I said.

"Bwana, please don't worry about Lindsey" he replied. "I promise I will look after her. Lindsey iko kama toto yangu." (Lindsey is like my child).

I could not watch Lindsey barking and crying and looking at me with sad eyes, so I told George to leave straight away. I did not care about leaving our possessions behind, but leaving Lindsey was too much for me.

Time was now running short, as I was leaving for Entebbe the same evening to catch my flight to London. I took one last look at my home and told my servants how sorry I was to have to leave my home and my country. I wished them all the best in the future. Both Gabriel and Margaret were in tears.

I was fortunate to get the airline booking confirmed for that evening. My suitcase was in my car and my airline ticket had been prepared a few weeks earlier.

I was used to the drive from Kampala to Entebbe and knew there was an army checkpoint in between the two towns. The army was harassing everybody passing the checkpoint, checking and opening suitcases, taking anything they liked from them and demanding money. When I got to the checkpoint they checked my suitcase, but fortunately they did not take anything. They did ask for money, leaving me no choice but to give them some of my allowance of £250. I was very worried about the army captain who had taken money from our office, as there was a strong chance that he would come looking for me. I prayed for my safe arrival at the airport.

As I parked my car at the airport, I realised that there was no-one left to take care of it. I took a paper and wrote on it "Anybody can take this car. The key is in the ignition". I checked in my suitcase. There was a two-hour wait before the flight took off, and they were the longest two hours of my life. There were army staff everywhere, and I was desperately worried that the army captain in dark glasses would reappear.

I kept on asking the airline staff if the flight was on time and when boarding would begin. They could see my anxiety. Don't worry, they said. The flight is on time and we will make the announcement as soon as we can.

At last came the announcement for passengers to board the flight. A few minutes later I was sitting in my seat, praying it would take off soon. Finally the aircraft took off, and I grinned with relief. The last thing I saw of Uganda was a heap of abandoned baggage lying on the runway.

CHAPTER SEVEN

ENGLAND: STARTING AGAIN

I was very sorry to leave Uganda, knowing that I would never be allowed to return. I had never thought of leaving before. I had loved every moment of my life there.

Jinny and our sons were staying with my sister-in-law Salu and her husband John in their flat at Harrow-on-the-Hill in North London, so I was not unduly worried about them. I was most grateful to Salu and John for looking after them, but the flat was full, so I could not go and live there as well.

My elder brother Arvind, who had moved to the UK long before, was living with his family in Kingsbury in North London. My eldest brother Shashi, his wife and his three daughters and son, all teenagers, had arrived in the UK during the earlier part of the exodus from Uganda. They were living with Arvind, so their house was full too. I phoned Arvind to get him to pick me up from London Heathrow. I was hoping he would put me up for few days at his place.

We arrived in England in mid September 1972. When we got to the airport there were other Ugandan Indians with us and we were told to get medical checks. Accommodation would then be arranged 'for any refugee who may need it'. I was stunned to hear the word 'refugee' as it sounded so degrading. I had often come to London on business trips, and had been met by someone smiling and welcoming me at the airport. This was all very different.

Arvind told me his house was full, but the airport authority would find me accommodation. When I asked them, they had difficulty finding somewhere for me to stay. In the end they manage to get me accommodation at an empty army barracks in Kensington. I gave the address to my brother, who volunteered to take me to Kensington.

When I arrived at the army camp, I found there were many Ugandan Indians living there. They were sharing two long halls, each with several beds. I did not expect this sort of accommodation and began to felt very much like a refugee. I made up my mind to get out as soon as I could. I went to see my family in Harrow, and found them living a difficult life in Salu's little flat. But Salu and John had been very kind to offer my family accommodation.

I could not stop thinking about Uganda. There were so many happy memories. The weather there was always so pleasant. Coming to the UK was a big culture shock, and I found the cold weather in October unbearable.

Starting a new life in England was very difficult. Of course, we had to do all our own housework. But at least we knew we were safe in the UK.

I had a small amount of money in my British bank account and we used it to buy woollens to keep us warm in the English winter. Soon we were looking for a house to rent. I managed to find a three-bedroom house in the Kenton area of North London. The landlord was an Indian who had originally come from Kenya, so he was very kind to us and gave us basic furniture like beds and cupboards.

Slowly we began to get used to England and to settle down. But it was very difficult to adjust to the English lifestyle. The days were getting shorter and it was dark by early afternoon. My younger son Sunil, who was now five, used to say "Dad, look it's dark, should we go to sleep now?" I would tell him it was too early because the nights in England at that time of year were much longer than they were back in Uganda, but this explanation did not satisfy him.

It was a complete change of life. In Uganda we had had our servants Gabriel and Margaret to do everything for us - our daily laundry, cleaning and cooking. We reminded ourselves that we were grateful to be alive. We had no choice but to force ourselves to start doing all the housework, cooking and so on. It was very hard, but there was no alternative. We had to become part of English society and behave as British citizens. It took us a long time.

Our first priority was to look for a school for our boys. We registered them for admission and the education authority found us a suitable school.

I felt a strong temptation to go back to Uganda and try to turn the clock back. We were missing our country so much, but we knew that the door was shut. It was impossible - we would never be able to go back after what had happened.

After we had been in England a few days, a letter came through the letterbox. It was from the National Front and read, "GO HOME - you don't belong here. GO BACK TO WHERE YOU CAME FROM!" This was a big shock, as we were doing our best to come to terms with our new home. I was afraid we might have to leave England and go back to the fear and stress of the Amin régime. I could not believe that a political party in England could be allowed to voice such a view (they would not now, of course). There was debate on television among all the political parties, including the National Front, about the Ugandan Indians and why so many of us had been allowed to come to England. This sort of discussion was making me more afraid for the future.

Whenever I saw soldiers or policemen on the streets, I felt a great fear of them and found myself instinctively praying that would not shoot us. The scars created by the soldiers of the Ugandan army stayed in my mind for a very long time.

My next task was to register myself with the British system and get a National Insurance number. My wife had done this, and she had got a job straight away with a travel agent in Edgware, so she guided me to a government office in Harrow. I got myself registered and was given a National Insurance number.

I was then told by this office to go and register myself for employment. I didn't understand this, but thought I had better follow the system. I told the government officer about my work experience and she said she would try to find a job for me, but she said it could be difficult as I had experience only with the aviation industry and there weren't many jobs in aviation. She was very kind and understanding. She told me to go to another office to get myself registered for a 'doll'. I was wondering, why do I need a doll?

I went to this office and joined a long queue of people. I asked the man behind me why we were all standing in a queue, and he explained that because I was unemployed the government would give me money – it was called the dole.

I felt very degraded when I was offered dole money, as I felt as if I was begging. It took me back to my schooldays, when I had been shamed because I was getting a free education. I went back to the employment officer and told her that the money was an insult and that I did not want it. I told her, you will soon see, I will find a job in the aviation industry.

Meanwhile my two partners had also left Uganda for the UK. I contacted one of them and he told me he was making arrangements to transfer money to the UK for the three of us to share. But when two of us went to see him, he gave us £2000 each and told us there was no more. We argued that this was not fair as we had all worked very hard in Uganda all our lives, but it had been very cleverly done by the finance director and there was nothing we could do.

I felt I had been robbed and had lost everything, in Uganda and now also in England. I burst into tears of helpless anger. But I had no choice but to bury my past and start a new life.

I decided to buy a car, but I was told by my neighbour that I might need a UK driving licence. When I checked with the authorities, I was told a Uganda driving licence was not acceptable in the UK and I would have to take a driving test.

Driving in Uganda was not as disciplined as in the UK, and the traffic cops were corruptible. I decided to take some driving lessons to get rid of the bad habits I had acquired there. The instructor told me that I must watch out for speed limit signs as I was driving too fast. I took his advice.

At my test, the examiner asked me a few questions and then we walked towards the car. He wanted to check my eyesight, so he pointed at a car and asked me to read out the registration number.

"There must be an easier way to get a driving licence," I said as we walked to the car to start the test.

"Like what?" he asked me.

"In Uganda you hand over money and they give you a licence" I said. "There is no need to go for a test."

He looked at me angrily. "Are you trying to bribe me?"

I realised I had annoyed him. "No!" I said. "Would I ever bribe you?"

"You make one mistake and I will fail you!" he said.

"Come on, would you do that to a refugee?"

"I was a refugee once" he said. "I came here from Hungary a few years ago. If I can make it, so can you."

I failed the test. When I asked him, why, he said I had not looked in the rear-view mirror before driving away. I told him I had, but he insisted.

The next time I made sure I did not see the same examiner. I passed.

Now I was ready to buy a car. I knew someone in Hounslow who was running a service station and dealing in second-hand cars. I went to see him and told him that I had only £250 to spend.

"That is a very small budget," he said. "But don't worry, I have just the car for you."

He showed me a white Hillman Husky with two side mirrors and a long flexible radio aerial, one end of which was clipped to the front of the roof. The body was dirty and had many rust spots.

"Don't worry, it works OK" said my friend. "Just go to the car accessory shop and buy a white spray paint and it will look as good as new."

I paid him the money. I wanted to take my family to come for a ride in our first English car, so I invited them to come for a spin. My son Sohail was not impressed.

"Dad, it looks terrible," he said.

"Don't worry, Sohail," I said. We will take it to the car wash, then we will buy that spray paint."

My wife looked at me very doubtfully.

"Do you know how to do this type of work?" she asked me.

"This is England," I said. "We are going to have to learn to do everything ourselves, like everyone else."

But I was very doubtful about my ability. In Uganda cars were washed by hand and the driver saw to it.

When we arrived at the car wash we watched for a while to see how it was done. Then I wound up the windows and drove in. When I tried to look into the side mirrors I realised that they had both fallen off the in the car wash. I stopped the car and we saw that the aerial had also fallen off.

We stopped the car and laughed our heads off. It seemed so funny. Then we went to the car shop and asked for a can of white spray. I sprayed paint on all the rusty spots without removing the rust first. Of course the new paint did not match the colour of the car, so it looked worse than before.

We drove the car off without waiting for the paint to dry, and when we got home the paintwork had all smudged.

"Look on the bright side" I told the family. "This car is a head turner." We all started laughing again.

I now started contacting various organisations connected with aviation and bought a copy of the trade newspaper. There was an interesting advertisement for a job at Heathrow, with a cargo logistics company. This was a company which was working as a handling company for various airlines, making up palettes with cargo supplied by the airline and then delivering the palette back to the airline. We had done this in Entebbe for Uganda Airlines. I applied for the position of office supervisor and was called for an interview. I was told I was over-qualified for the position, but they offered it to me anyway.

Working as a mere supervisor was a big comedown for me, as I had been managing director of a cargo logistics company in Uganda, but for now I had to swallow my pride. I had to accept that I lacked experience in the UK.

While I had been living in Uganda I had often travelled to England to meet airline executives. I would stay in a good hotel and fly back as soon as the business was done. I soon found that living in England as a resident was very different. In Uganda everything was casual and easy-going. In England everything was very calculated and programmed and people were cold in their attitude. It was very hard to get used to this, but like many Ugandan

Indians I forced myself to accept the new way of life and become part of English society instead of thinking of how life had been in Uganda.

I was now getting a weekly salary, so I bought some flowers, went to the employment office and gave them to the lady I'd seen. I told her they were a small gift for being so nice to me and I had bought them with my first English pay-packet. She was speechless. "I wish everybody was like you," she said.

Three months after I had started my new job, the manager called me in and said he was promoting me to assistant manager and giving me a company car. I was the only Indian on the staff and there was some resentment about my promotion, particularly from one of the other supervisors. When we were all in the pub during the lunch break, he said he resented an immigrant coming to his country and taking someone's job. Naturally I was not going to accept this.

"You know, because I am a little darker than you I have to be three times smarter and more experienced than you to get promoted like this in such a short time" I said. There was a moment of silence, and then some of my colleagues clapped in appreciation of what I had said.

We were looking for more airlines to give us work. At that time there was an African airline called Simba Air, a subsidiary of Kenya airways, which operated regular cargo flights between Nairobi and Heathrow. I had a chat with the manager and asked him if we would be interested in handling the extra business. The manager was encouraging and asked me to try and get the Simba Air contract. I knew the boss in Nairobi, who frequently used to visit London on business, so I rang him and persuaded him to give the contract to us. We would load cargo on aircraft palettes and then deliver the palettes to the airline concerned.

A few months later one of the directors of our company asked me to come to his office. He told me they had decided to promote me to General Manager. I told the director that I didn't want to take away someone's job, and the present General Manager was my friend and had always been very nice to me, so I did not want to accept the offer. The director told me that if I did not take the job it would go to someone else, and the present General Manager was aware of the situation.

I said I would speak to the man and let the director know. The manager told me he appreciated my loyalty, and that he was leaving anyway as he was emigrating to the USA. My conscience was now clear, so I took up the position as General Manager.

Now that Jinny and I were settled in our jobs, I decided we should buy a house. We found a suitable one in Edgware, and found a good school there for Sohail and Sunil. Economically our life was going well, but Jinny and I now started to have problems in our relationship. It is very strange how going through the most difficult times can affect a couple; it can either create a closer relationship or make it all fall apart. We tried to work everything out, but there was continuous friction between us and it started affecting our children. Since we just could not get along with each other, we decided to split up. We divorced in 1974 and I left the house to Jinny so that my children would live comfortably.

I moved in with a friend in Kenton and for a while I stayed with his family as a paying guest. That was very hard. But in 1975 I married again, to Ranjna, and started a new life. After a few months we moved from Kenton to Southall. Soon Ranjna joined us to work with my company, and then a few months later she got a job with the East African Airways cargo office at Heathrow.

I made a point of seeing my boys every weekend. However it wasn't long before Jinny met another man, Hadi, and they got married and decided to move to Canada. The Canadian Embassy gave them permission, but I had to confirm that I had no objection to my sons going to live in Canada. I was very reluctant, as I knew I would not be able to see them very often, but I knew that in many ways Canada would give them a better life than the UK, so I signed the document.

My new wife Ranjna and I were determined to move forward with our lives. We had to get out of Southall. We managed to buy a small house in Hillingdon with two and half bedrooms. We were very happy to be able to move into a place of our own.

I was now thinking about starting my own business. I got in touch with my old contacts from the Indian community in the UK, people who like me had come there as part of the exodus of Ugandan Indians. They were happy to hear from me, and they were all involved in exporting to East Africa and other countries. Five companies were willing to give me their support and all encouraged me to start a business. Ranjna was working with Kenya Airways in their cargo department at Heathrow, so we had her income to fall back on while my business became established.

I needed some working capital, so I asked my bank manager for a loan. He asked me if I could offer them any collateral. I could not, of course, so I said I would give him my word that I would pay back every penny. In Uganda that would have been good enough, but not for my English bank manager. He turned me down. In fact he told me I was making a very big blunder trying to start a cargo logistics business, because there were many such firms around Heathrow and there would be too much competition. Instead he suggested I open a little shop selling newspapers, magazines and cigarettes – this way the bank could give me a small loan.

I was very disappointed that the bank manager thought that because I was Indian all I could do was run a corner shop. I told him that within six months I would prove him wrong.

I was determined to start my business even without the bank's help. I asked my mother for a loan. All she had was £100, which would just cover the cost of setting up a company. I had another £100 in my personal account.

I started Courcan International Cargo Ltd in 1976. I got some stationery printed and opened a bank account with an £80 deposit.

At first it was extremely difficult. I bought a cheap typewriter and worked from home. One of those who had encouraged me to start the business was a very good friend who was a regular exporter to East Africa. I told him I was ready do business with him, but because I had no working capital I could not give him a credit facility. This customer was very good to me; he agreed to pay me in advance. His help was a godsend. I had similar support from my other four customers, and slowly business started to build.

We needed a warehouse facility to receive the cargo, so I made an arrangement with a warehouse company not far from home to receive it, weigh it and report to me. From this information I prepared the export documents. I arranged with a transport company to deliver the cargo. Ranjna joined me each evening after coming home from her daytime job and we worked late nights and early mornings together.

As the business started flourishing, Ranjna left her job with Kenya Airways to help me. We bought a small car. Many a time we had to make more than one drop, and it was costly to hire transport repeatedly, so when this happened we used to hire a van, go to the warehouse late at night, load the van and deliver the cargo to the various airlines before returning the van.

Soon we had to rent a small office near the airport and employ a couple of staff to help us. All export business was done on a CIF (cost, insurance and freight) basis only – the cost of the goods, the insurance and the freight were all rolled together.

I found it very difficult to get new business, as none of the English exporters would give me a contract. This was because the exporters had complete control of their exports and would use only their nominated cargo agents. So I had to be innovative again. I thought of persuading the importer to pay the carriage charges at their end when they received the goods. This would enable them to control their charges.

I went to Nairobi to try to persuade the importers to introduce this new but sensible approach. I explained that the exporter has no automatic right to make additional profit from the importer on carriage charges. Also, customs duty is charged on the value of the goods plus the carriage, so when the carriage charges were paid by the importer there was a saving in duty. The importers were very happy with this idea.

I was also handling some small-scale exports to Uganda, but I could not go to my old country in person because of what had happened to me there. Not that there was much need, as the economy was in very bad shape since the Indian business people had left.

Since my approach of consignee selling was so successful, I decided to go to Tanzania and make some contacts there. I flew to Dar es Salaam, the principal city of Tanzania, and sold the new concept with great success.

One day while she was working at Kenya Airways, Ranjna came across a customer who was desperately looking for a good cargo agent in London. She gave him my phone number and he called me, insisting on seeing me straight away in my office. He was from a town called Mwanza, the second largest town in Tanzania. His transactions were small but complicated to handle, and he was asking for more than the usual service provided by the cargo agent.

I agreed to give his business my personal attention. When after a few months his company won big contracts and expanded its business, I got a great opportunity to handle their complete air and sea import business. Other importers in Mwanza also started giving me business.

We now acquired a bigger office and took a warehouse in Uxbridge on a long lease. We started doing export business both by air and sea to worldwide destinations. I was travelling non-stop to see my customers. Besides doing business in East Africa, we started providing services to other countries, including Nigeria, Zaire, Zambia, Malawi and South Africa.

I have many stories to tell of my travels in Africa. There was the time I had to travel to Zaire to see a couple of contacts there who were prepared to introduce me to some new contacts in Kinshasa, the capital. I needed a visa, which I got from the Zaire Embassy in London. I booked my flight to Kinshasa, which I had never visited before, and on my arrival at the immigration desk the office spoke to me in French. I could not understand the officer and told him I could only speak English (they do not speak Swahili in Zaire). The officer spoke to me in broken English.

"Your visa is no good," he said. I asked him what was wrong with it and told him I had got it from his country's embassy in London.

"The signature is no good," he said.

There was a Belgian standing behind me listening to our conversation, and he tapped my shoulder and told me the officer wanted money. Now I understood. I gave the officer £10. He was happy with that and told me my visa was now good, and he stamped my passport.

The market in Nigeria was big, with many goods being imported from the UK. We were trading with three customers In Lagos and Kano, and I asked if they could introduce me to more customers in Nigeria. Two of them agreed to help me and said I must visit Lagos.

I was well aware of the notorious immigration and customs officers in Lagos. If your passport and health documents were in order you would have no problems, but if anything was wrong they regarded it as a great opportunity to extract money from the passenger. They would point out the mistake and ask for 'dash', meaning a bribe.

A regular traveller told me that the first time he went to Lagos, the health officer asked him for his yellow fever certificate. He handed it over, and it promptly disappeared. Once again the health officer asked the man for his yellow fever certificate.

"I just gave it to you!" said the traveller.

"Sorry, you have not given me any certificate," said the health officer. "If you don't have the health certificate I will not let you into Nigeria."

The traveller was angry.

"OK" he said. "If you are not going to allow me in, let me have my suitcase back so I can go back home!"

The officer laughed at him. "You are not allowed into Nigeria, but your suitcase is allowed in!" he said. Of course the man had to bribe him, and his yellow fever certificate miraculously reappeared. In a situation like this it is best not to try to demand your rights. You have to negotiate.

For outgoing passengers, the airline check-in desk used to have a board displaying the flight number. You would go and queue up at the desk where your flight number was displayed and perhaps wait for hours. Sometimes, without warning, a member of staff would appear, remove the board displaying the flight number and move it to another position. Everyone would run to the new position and lose their places in the queue. There would be chaos and everyone would start arguing over their place in the queue.

The flights from Lagos to London were always full in those days. You would check in your luggage and get a boarding pass long before the boarding time. The airline staff always used to overbook the flight and give boarding passes to the unconfirmed passengers in return for bribes. When the flights was announced, all the passengers with the boarding passes would run to the aircraft to make sure they got their seat before someone else took it. The passengers who did not get seats were told to wait for another flight. Complaining was a waste of time. It was a system driven by corruption, and we all just had to learn to live with it.

Once I was in Lagos staying with a friend. I decided to go to Lome in Togo for a day and spend another day in Lagos before returning to London. Since I was coming back to Lagos, I left my return ticket to London and a small suitcase at my friend's home. I did not need a visa to travel to Nigeria, so I thought I was safe travelling back from Lome to Lagos.

On my arrival at Lagos Airport the immigration officer asked me to show him my onward ticket from Lagos to London. I said I had left it in Lagos. The officer looked at me and said "dash time!"

I pointed out that the last time I had travelled the same way there had been no problem. The officer looked at me and said I either had to show him my ticket or buy another. I had to give him his bribe. Travelling to Nigeria was always very stressful.

My experience of travelling in East Africa was always very smooth, except for the first time I arrived at Dar es Salaam from London. The health officer asked me for a yellow fever certificate, since I was coming from England. It was in order, but he said the date of the vaccination was incorrect, so he would to give me another injection. I was not prepared to pay the officer any money and told him to give me the vaccination. We went to his office and he took a metal box out from his desk. The box was rusty and inside were two hypodermic needles stuck to each other with rust.

"Surely you are not going to use this on me?" I said.

"These are the only needles I have" he replied. I had no choice but to give him money.

Back in England, one of my staff came to tell me that our Italian associate in Milan was not co-operating. Our customer was very annoyed with us as his consignment had not arrived in London. The agent had been promising dispatch for the past two days, but he kept letting us down and it had not arrived.

I called the agent.

"Umberto!" I said. "Where is this urgent consignment for our customer in London?"

"Good morning Sam" he said.

"Umberto, it is not a good morning!" I said. "After two days you have still not dispatched this urgent consignment."

"Ask me where is Alberto?" replied Umberto.

"Who is Alberto?"

"He is my cousin."

"We are looking for an urgent consignment and you are talking to me about Alberto?"

"Alberto is at the airport to see personally that the consignment leaves today," he said.

"Umberto, you said the same thing to my staff yesterday" I replied.

"Yesterday was yesterday, but I swear on my mother's grave the consignment is leaving today?" he answered.

"I know your family, Umberto," I said. "Your mother is alive!"

"OK it is my mother-in-law, but it is the same thing" he said. "Don't worry Sam, I promise you the consignment is on board now on Alitalia."

We were lucky. At last the consignment arrived at the airport.

CHAPTER EIGHT

RETURN TO UGANDA

I had been travelling regularly on business to Kenya and Tanzania, but I was not prepared to go Uganda again while Amin was still in power. However I very much wanted to see the country again when I could and to visit my old friends in Kampala. I longed to see my house again and drive to the places I had known so well. I was also keen to do business with Uganda. I always followed the news and took a great interest in developments there.

Amin's rule had been a total disaster for Uganda. His régime was blamed for killing some 300,000 people and the economy was in ruins. By 1978 he had become an international outcast and his remaining supporters had largely deserted him.

Amin himself had become increasingly deluded and megalomaniacal. His full self-bestowed title was His Excellency President for Life, Field Marshal Al Hadji Doctor Idi Amin Dada, VC, DSO, MC, CBE, Lord of the Beasts of the Earth and Fishes of the Sea and Conqueror of the British Empire in Africa in General and Uganda in Particular, in addition to the claim, made famous by a recent film, that he was the uncrowned King of Scotland.

Julius Nyerere, the Tanzanian President, had a very good relationship with Milton Obote, the ex-Prime Minister of Uganda, who was living in exile there. Many soldiers from Uganda had fled to Tanzania to join Obote. The exiled soldiers tried to overthrow Amin, but were not successful.

Amin's final mistake was to send troops into Tanzania to try to claim part of it. The Tanzanian army, helped by the exiled Ugandan soldiers, retaliated and invaded Uganda, and Amin was forced to flee to Libya and seek sanctuary with his ally Colonel Gaddafi. Later he moved to Saudi Arabia, where he died in 2003. One of his wives had pleaded with the then Ugandan leader, President Museveni, for her husband to be allowed to spend his last days in his homeland, but Museveni retorted that he would have to answer for his sins first.

After Amin was finally sent packing, Milton Obote came back to power and brought back the civilian government. But the country was bankrupt and in chaos, and nothing was working. It was a huge task for the new government to rebuild the country's ruined economy.

The Uganda Government Office in London invited Ugandan Asians to a meeting. We were being asked to go back to help to get the country back on its feet. We were told that we could have our old homes back if we would move back there. The meeting was not very successful, as nine years on most of the Asians had become settled in the UK and were doing well. Nine years is a long time, and they were not prepared to start all over again in Uganda.

I did however very much want to see my home country, and my long-awaited opportunity to return had now arrived. In January 1981 I was due to make one of my regular trips to Kenya and Tanzania, and I thought the time was right to go and see my old country. I had a very good friend, Zul, who was still living in Kampala, and I asked him if it was safe for me to visit. Zul told me I should not worry. I told him I was planning to book myself a room in a good hotel, but he said the hotels were not yet properly organised for guests and I should stay with him in his house in the Kololo area. He said his driver would pick me up from the airport.

I took a flight from Nairobi to Entebbe. I was very excited about seeing my home country again, but I also felt very afraid and on edge, because of all that had happened there. Five years before, my airport had been the focus of world attention when it was the scene of the notorious Operation Entebbe. An Air France airliner was hijacked by Palestinian terrorists and flown to the airport. An Israeli force rescued almost all of them and severely upset Idi Amin, who had backed the hostages, by destroying most of his fighter planes and killing many of his soldiers.

When my flight landed at Entebbe airport and I climbed down the steps, I found I had a reception committee. Some of the people I had worked with at the airport had come to welcome me. They came running towards me, full of excitement. There were tears running down their faces. They were very happy to see me after such a long time, and I was just as happy to see them.

I was escorted to the immigration desk, where more staff came out to see me.

"Sir, welcome back!" said one. "We are so happy to see you. We would all like to come back to work for your company in Entebbe and Kampala."

I had to break the news gently to them that I was not returning to Uganda.

"But Bwana, this is your country, we need your help!" said one of them. I had great difficulty controlling my emotions.

"I am sorry, my home is England now" I said. "I am only here to do some business with Uganda from England." They were all very disappointed.

My friend Zul's driver came to take me to Kampala. The road was in terrible condition, and it took us much more than the usual half hour to cover the 20 miles. It was just as bad in Kampala, but even so I was very happy to see those streets again after nine long years away.

Kololo has always been an upmarket area with beautiful houses. When we reached my friend's home it was still only 11 am, so I had the day in front of me. The driver gave me the keys to a car and said Zul wanted me to have the use of it while I was there. He would be home that evening.

Then a water tanker appeared with a supply of fresh water. This was a strange sight, as I had never seen such a thing in Uganda before, and there had never been any shortage of water. I asked Zul's cook why there was a water tanker, and he explained that the pump systems were not working. Nothing was working.

I felt very excited at being able to spend the day exploring around Kampala. I drove straight away to Mackenzie Vale, to see the house I had lived in. I parked my car opposite the house and was disappointed to see that the garden was full of weeds. It was an emotional experience to see the house, but I pushed my feelings away and drove away towards the city. There I went for a walk and started looking for familiar faces. I went to see my old office on Entebbe Road, and found only one person working there. She did not know me. I introduced myself to her and asked about my old colleague Omako. She said he would be arriving shortly and invited me to wait for him in the office.

When Omako appeared we were both very happy to see each other. I asked him how business was going and he said there was nothing much for them to do, as they were hardly getting any business.

At the end of the day I drove to my friend's home. Zul was waiting for me, and it was nice to see him after such a long time. He offered me any help I needed, and I told him I would be staying three or four days to explore the possibilities for doing business before going on to Nairobi.

After dinner we talked late into the night before turning in. At about two in the morning I was awoken by the sound of shooting coming from far away. I felt very scared, as the sound took me back to my last days in Uganda. I woke Zul up and asked him what was going on, and he said I should not worry as the sounds were coming from the army barracks. Zul was perhaps used to the sound of guns, but to me it was a sign that the problems in Uganda were not yet over. I could not sleep the rest of the long night, as I kept on getting flashbacks to my bad experiences. They seemed so real in my mind and was worried that history could repeat itself. I could not wait for daylight to come.

Over breakfast I told Zul that I was not prepared to stay any longer in Uganda. I felt very scared and wanted to fly to Nairobi that day. Zul tried hard to persuade me and kept telling me I should not worry and I should leave my past behind me, but I could not. I was not convinced, as I could not help my feelings. I kept on getting flashbacks of my past experiences with Amin's soldiers.

I booked my flight to Nairobi and left for Entebbe airport the same day.

Arriving safely in Nairobi gave me a great feeling of relief. I stayed there three days and met my regular customers and some new contacts as well.

It was nice to come back to Uganda, but I had returned too soon. In 1981 it was less than two years since Amin had been deposed, and the country was still in turmoil. I should not have expected to find the Uganda I had known. It would take much longer for the new government to sort out the mess and make a new beginning.

It was time for me to go back home. I was happy to return to my family and the safe environment of England.

One day I had an appointment to meet a businessman from Kenya who was staying at the Cumberland Hotel in London. With him was a friend from Uganda, who was introduced to me as Joseph. We were talking away, and after a while the businessman left us to see someone else in another hotel. Joseph and I had an interesting discussion about the good old days in Kampala. Joseph mentioned to me that he was looking for a cargo agent, as he was exporting books to Uganda. When I told him I was a cargo agent and might be able to help him, we arranged to meet in my office the next day.

We started to do business with Joseph to help him to export his books to Uganda. One night I invited him for dinner. Since he was living in London, my wife and I took him to an Italian restaurant in Chelsea.

This was a very classy restaurant. Joseph asked for prawn cocktail as a starter and then for his main course he ordered a big steak with French fries and vegetables. My wife and I had pasta.

After the main course we decided to order desserts. After the dessert the waiter asked if we would like coffee, but to our great surprise Joseph asked for another steak. This was embarrassing both for us and the waiter. The waiter asked Joseph if he was sure he wanted another steak. I quickly intervened and told the waiter that if Joseph wanted the steak, he must have one.

The restaurant was closing and the waiter was very keen to go home, but

Joseph was taking his time, enjoying his second steak and chatting away with us. The waiter was hovering around the table and coming very close to Joseph's seat, obviously wanting to take his plate away. This made Joseph very irritated. He told me the waiter was getting on his nerves and trying to take away his dinner. He kept his eyes on the waiter and every time the waiter came near he would protect his plate with his hands.

Ranjna and I found this hilarious, but we had to keep straight faces and not burst out laughing in front of Joseph. In the end he won the battle of nerves and enjoyed finishing his steak.

Our company was doing well with its exports to Africa. Now I wanted to move further and spread our wings to other worldwide destinations. South East Asia seemed a promising area, as there was a good possibility of imports from Thailand, Hong Kong and Korea. Through our agent's network I decided to visit all three.

My first stop was Bangkok. It was a long flight from London, so I decided to fly on Friday and rest over the weekend. I told the taxi driver to come back and take me sightseeing on the Sunday.

The driver turned up bang on time. "It was laning last night" he said. I did not understand him, so I asked him to explain what 'laning' was.

"Laning, laning!" he said, throwing his arms in the air and shaking his hands downward.

"Oh, you mean raining!" I said.

"Yes, laning!"

He took me to see the temple of Buddha, and on the way he pointed to a statue of a soldier and said "Militili molument!" I managed not to burst out laughing.

I met my associates and some customers on the Monday and after three days I went on to Hong Kong and Seoul. My trip was successful, and after a few days I flew back to England.

After coming back from South East Asia I was introduced to someone who was exporting machinery and electronic parts by air to Mexico City.

He wanted to try to do some business with us, as his logistics agent in the UK did not have a very good associate in Mexico and the service level was poor. An associate agent in Mexico was recommended to us by another agent from Germany, and he turned out to be a good one. The service he provided was excellent, and business proved much better than we had expected.

After sending a few consignments to Mexico City I decided to pay a visit there to try to increase the business between the UK and Mexico. I arrived at Mexico City airport to find myself in a long building with many desks next to each other and immigration officers sitting behind each desk. As an Indian with a long droopy moustache, I must have looked to the immigration officer like a Mexican, and he started speaking to me in Spanish. I apologised to him and explained that I could only speak English. I could see from the expression on the man's face that he did not believe me. He turned to the immigration officer on his right and said something in Spanish – I knew they were talking about me but I could not understand what they were saying. The person standing behind me said I was pretending to be an 'Americano' and did not want to speak Spanish. I just kept quiet and left the immigration hall.

Here I was greeted by my associate and taken to my hotel. I told him what had happened, and he said he did not blame the officers because I looked so much like a Mexican. He said I would have this problem everywhere, as people would think I was a local and speak to me in Spanish. He was right. Everyone I met tried to speak Spanish to me.

This was only my first visit, so I did not expect to find new customers so soon. I simply enjoyed meeting new people in a new country. I noticed that Mexicans took a very casual approach to business.

I decided that the next time I visited East Africa I would go on from Nairobi to Dar es Salaam, Tanga and Arusha, in Tanzania. It was a very successful trip. I made Dar es Salaam my last stop. I had arranged a meeting with some customers there before taking a British Airways flight back to London.

Our company had been having difficulties getting cargo space on British

Airways, as there was a shortage of available room on their planes. Much of the space was taken up with catering equipment, food and drink, which had to be flown to various destinations and kept there to feed the returning passengers. Their catering requirements were taking priority and leaving very little space for other paying cargo. What little space they had was sold to us at a premium price.

During the flight from Dar es Salaam to London I watched the flight crew serving drinks and meals to the passengers and thought about the problem. We wanted to use British Airways for very urgent consignments on non-stop flights, as they had more destinations for these than any other airline.

I had an idea - to offer to send BA's non-paying revenue items, catering equipment and drinks on other airlines and charter flights at a lower airfreight rate. This would give them extra cargo space, which could be used to fly urgent cargo at the premium rate. British Airways was very happy with this idea, and we went ahead. The new system brought us a lot of business to many destinations, and we had to employ more staff to provide them with the required premium service. Business was going very well.

CHAPTER NINE

THE CHALLENGE OF INDIA

By 1979 I had been building my cargo company for three years. The horizons of our business had become very much wider and we were flying to and from many more destinations. We were even dealing with a few Asian countries, but we were not yet doing any business with India. This seemed a serious omission, given that my wife and I were both of Indian origin and could read, write and speak both Gujarati and Hindi.

Unfortunately neither of us had any relatives in India. Nor had either of us ever been there. We decided it was high time to put that right by visiting the land of our fathers. We estimated that we would need three weeks in India to see all that we wanted to see, and finally we managed to squeeze in time from our busy lives and booked to fly to Bombay in December 1979. We were very excited about the trip.

We arrived at Bombay airport in the early morning, feeling very tired. There was a long queue at the immigration counter and it was chaotic. We had to fill in the Indian immigration form before joining the queue, as no-one had given us one in the aircraft.

At last we had completed our forms, joined the queue and were slowly getting closer to the desk. But as we approached, the immigration officer pointed to a European family who were queuing behind us and gestured to them to come to the counter. He was inviting them to jump ahead of us.

I could not tolerate this blatant discrimination and asked the officer why he was asking them to take our place. He said they were visitors, so they should be given priority. I had heard from many of our UK friends that Europeans were given special attention when they came to India, but this was happening right in front of our eyes.

I objected strongly and told the officer that this was discrimination and that in any case the European family were no different from us, as we were visitors too. The officer was not happy, but he had no choice but to attend to us first. The Europeans were embarrassed and told us they were quite prepared to wait for their turn. I told them it was not their fault, and we agreed that it was astonishing how these Indian officials could discriminate against their own people.

We were booked at the Taj Hotel, and were amazed to see how beautiful it was. Some friends who were staying in Bombay came to see us the next day and offered us to take us around the city. We had a lot of fun with them and visited many places. Then it was on to Delhi, the Indian capital. The hotel arranged for a guided tour and we visited many historical places and very much enjoyed Delhi.

From Delhi we went by train to Agra to see the great Taj Mahal, one of the wonders of the world. It was breathtaking. We continued on to Jaipur and Udaipur and from there we went to Aurangabad. Then it was on to Goa, which we also thoroughly enjoyed, with its sunshine, sand and sea. It was a great holiday. We enjoyed all the places we visited. Finally we came back to England, laden with shopping.

After seeing India I was keen to do business there, because I could see a very big market. I knew a businessman from East Africa who was living in Bombay, so I contacted him and asked him about it. He discouraged me from trying to do business in Bombay and said there were many difficulties and restrictions. You needed all sorts of government licences, he said, and customs duty was very high. Exporting goods from India was easier than importing, but even exporting involved government formalities. Basically, India was not an open market.

I was a little disappointed and decided to check out the import regulations. As a cargo agent I could see a very big opportunity for shipping goods to India, as so many products were not available there.

We came back home with many good memories of India. I decided not to pursue doing business with India just yet, but hoped that one day she would open her markets, and then I would go there again and look for opportunities.

Then one day I was lucky enough to meet an exporter in England who was regularly sending his merchandise to Bombay. I contacted this man and managed to break the ice, as he agreed to let me handle his airfreight. It was a small piece of business, but I saw it as my opportunity to open a door to doing business with India.

I continued with my usual business with the rest of the world, but the possibility of trading with India was always in my mind. I would just have to wait for the opportunity.

In the early 1980s I read in the English newspapers that the Government of India was inviting NRIs (non-resident Indians) to come to India and take part in business there. I saw this as a very big opportunity. I decided not to wait any longer before trying to develop trade with India.

Experience had taught me that if you have a good and workable plan, you should not put it on the shelf. You should do your homework, then put the idea into action as soon as you can.

I decided to start with Bombay, as the leading commercial centre. I could speak the local language, Hindi, and I believe that speaking the same language quickly enables you to get closer to people.

I contacted the only Indian importer in Bombay, which had two partners, Mr Pansari and Mr Choudhary, and asked for their advice and help in introducing me to other importers in Bombay. They were very honest with me. They said they themselves were new to the import business and had a very small company, so they did not have any contacts to introduce to me. Instead, they said, why didn't I come to Bombay, and perhaps I would be able to meet some new importers.

I was determined to win new business by offering our cargo logistics service to importers in Bombay. I could see a huge new market opening for importers in India, as well as for UK and European companies exporting to India.

I had to find the right firms, which was a big challenge. I contacted the commercial attaché of the Indian Embassy in London to seek the names of firms who were importing goods to Bombay. They could only give me contacts for exporters, which was not want I wanted. I then contacted the British Ministry of Commerce, who gave me some names of importers in Bombay, but they could not tell me any other information related to my trade, such as whether they were imported by sea or air.

I was not prepared to travel to Bombay without doing any homework first. I decided to send a mailshot, and sent letters to about 100 importers in Bombay introducing my company to them and asking them to fill in a form asking the relevant questions. To my surprise I received about 15 replies from people who were willing to meet me in Bombay. This was a great achievement for me.

I already had a contact with an Indian cargo agent, so I got in touch with them and prepared to fly to Bombay to meet them. I tried to make an appointment with each importer, but the reply from them was always the same – come to Bombay, contact us and we will arrange to meet you. This seemed a very casual approach. I decided not to worry about it and accept it as their way of life. But I did appreciate receiving those replies, as I knew that if I had tried the same thing in Europe I would have received no response at all.

It was 1986 when I arrived in Bombay on business for the first time. I found a very different India from the one we had seen on holiday in 1979. This time I had a different mind-frame. I was full of curiosity and ambition to do business with my countrymen. I hoped it would be easier to do business speaking the local language and having the same culture.

It was very early morning when I arrived in the biggest city in the largest democratic country in the world. I booked myself into the Taj President hotel, as this hotel was in the heart of the trading area of Bombay.

The first thing I noticed was the way the hotel staff kept nodding their heads to say yes, the way we do when saying no. The hotel porter who took my baggage and escorted me to my room kept doing it while I was talking to him. I couldn't work out whether he was saying yes or no. When I asked him about it, he said, "Sir, I am saying yes". This was something new to me, as in the rest of the world people nod from left to right a couple of times to indicate no, so you can see it is different from yes. This method of saying yes was a new one for me.

Local Indians would stare at me, so I asked them why. They said it was because I was a foreigner

"How can you tell?" I asked one of them. "I am an Indian!"

"Yes you are Indian, but you are not from India, you look different, we can tell" he said.

All very puzzling, but I was very excited and optimistic that I would do some positive business in such a huge market.

Next morning I started phoning my contacts. The first person I rang was very happy to hear from me, saying welcome to India. I asked him for a convenient time to meet him in his office.

"Sir, you can come any time," he said. I realised he was being very polite and telling me he could accommodate me at my convenience. My thinking was more European, so I asked him again what time would be convenient, and again he said I could come any time and would be most welcome. This was difficult for me as I was used to fixing a precise time.

"How about 11 am today?" I asked him. He agreed to that. Then I phoned the rest of my contacts, but in every case I ran into difficulties. I would be told that the person I wanted was not in the office and no-one knew when he would be back. I was always invited to try later and told I would be most welcome to come and see the man.

I was now getting late for my first appointment, so I decided to move on. For the rest of the appointments I decided to do crash calls, as everybody had such a casual approach. I would just walk into their offices.

I gave the taxi driver the address of the customer and asked him if he knew the way. He nodded his head, and drove me to the correct street and told me we had arrived.

"You are here sir," he said.

"So where is this address I am looking for?" I asked him.

"Sir, I know the street, but how am I to know which building?" he replied.

"I gave you the office address with the number of the building," I said. "You are saying you don't know where it is?"

"No sir, I do not."

In those days there were no mobile phones of course, so I told the driver to take me back to the hotel. I returned very frustrated and annoyed with the taxi driver, because I was now late for my appointment. I rang the customer and apologised for the delay, but he was very casual about it.

"You have to give them a landmark," he said. "Tell them our office building is opposite the customs office. I will be waiting for you."

I realised that giving a full address with a pin code did not mean anything to the taxi driver - the landmark was much more important than the postal address. The landmark has to be a building which is known to most people and certainly to the taxi driver. "Opposite" the landmark may not mean opposite - it could be behind it, or just near it.

At last I arrived for my appointment and the secretary showed me to the office of my prospective customer. His first act was to offer me a glass of water. I was afraid of drinking the Bombay water, so I politely refused it. Instead they offered me the choice of tea or a cold drink. I asked for tea, but unfortunately they put a lot of sugar in it, and I drink tea without sugar. However, I pretended to drink it, as I thought it would be rude to ask for it without sugar.

I started with a casual discussion, instead of talking shop straight away. But after a while I realised that the customer was not really interested in doing business. He had just wanted to meet me, as he had never met an Indian from overseas. He wanted to see how I talked and watch my body language. He was very curious to learn anything I could tell him about business in England.

I thought of telling him how unfair he was to call me all the way from England and pretend to be a big importer. I mentioned the form I had sent him, on which he had told me how much he was regularly importing. He explained that this was the amount he was hoping to import.

I decided to keep cool, and concluded our unfruitful meeting. I was not just annoyed but worried, because I was afraid the rest of my contacts would turn out the same and my trip to Bombay would be wasted. However I pushed away all these negative thoughts and went to my second appointment. I telephoned the second contact from the first man's office and got the details, including the all-important landmark to give to the taxi-driver.

I was beginning to understand the new import market. As doors were opening many Indian companies were interested in getting into this huge new field and looking for a 'piece of the action'. I began to realise that the person across the table might look like me, but his thinking and approach were quite different. I decided to start thinking like an Indian, to try to be the part of the local business society, rather than using my European approach. I was here to do business, so I had better change my way of thinking rather than try to convert them. I would give the market what it wanted, instead of patronising them and trying to offer a service my way.

I also realised that the cultural divide between East and West is very wide. The differences between the two societies are considerable, and neither wanted to change. I believed strongly that to be successful in relationships between two societies both had to come halfway to shorten the cultural bridge. Then doing business would be easy, and we would not get bogged down in frustration and end up going home empty handed.

India is like Europe, with many countries and many languages in one country and different culture and food from one region to another. To give a simple example, most westerners think all curries are simply Indian, but they vary greatly according to the method of cooking and the spices used, which are different in each region.

I also realised that in the East they were much more flexible about profit margins. In the West we tended to keep our margins at a set figure, say 10% or 15%. We preferred to stick by the margin, even if it scared away the customer, instead of lowering it to get the business. In other words, we in the West were less prepared to think about working with a small profit margin on a large turnover. In India, businesses were based on a small profit margin with a large turnover. Some Indian businessman would do business without any profit at all, if it kept the customer happy, so he would come back and buy another product on which a profit could be made.

I decided to accept the Indian approach instead of making a fuss and sticking to my western way. Otherwise I would simply be wasting my time and money in India.

I hailed another taxi and gave the address and landmark of the second contact to the driver, who found the right address quickly. This company was bigger than the first one. The receptionist asked me to have a seat in the waiting area and someone came and offered me a glass of water; once again I politely refused, so she offered me tea and I asked for it without sugar.

While I was drinking my tea a woman came to meet me and asked me to follow her to the manager's office, which was a glass cubicle. I could see another visitor in the cubicle, so I was a little reluctant to enter, as I did not want to invade anyone's privacy. But the lady assured me it was OK to go in.

The manager invited me to take a seat. I sat by the other visitor. The manager offered me a tea. I said I had just had one, but he said it was ok to have another tea with them and ordered one for me.

"After all, you have come from England" he said. "At least I must offer you a cup of tea. You are a guest and most welcome in India." Then he started talking to me, instead of finishing the discussion with the visitor.

I found it a little odd to start talking business with another visitor present. The other man was drinking his tea and making a slurping noise. I was getting irritated with this, but I kept smiling. As before, I tried to talk about India, but my prospect was more interested in finding out about England. I got a little concerned, and hoped this man would not turn out like the first one.

My thoughts were interrupted by the lady who had escorted me to the manager's office. She barged into the cubicle.

"Sir" she said. "I have managed to get that important call through to our Bangalore office, the one I have been trying for three days. It is through now, can you please speak to them?" The manager picked up his phone and started shouting at the top of his voice. In those days telecommunications in India were very bad and people had to shout so that they could hear each other.

As he was engaged in this important telephone discussion, the manager saw a man passing and called out to him

"Ramlal!" he shouted. "Did you manage to complete that job?"

Meanwhile the phone discussion was going on and we could all hear what the Bangalore office was saying. Ramlal came into the office to talk to the manager, nodding more aggressively than normal to show he agreed with his manager.

To me this was all hilarious. There was chaos in that little office, with five of us all talking at once. I could not understand why the other visitor was still sitting there, as all this took a long time, but I could see he was very curious and was listening to our discussion. I was holding on to myself to stop myself from bursting out laughing at the chaos and confusion.

Finally, when all this was over, the visitor got up, politely shook hands with all of us and left. I was happy he had gone, as I felt I could now have some privacy.

The manager looked at me and asked me to start the discussion from the beginning. I patiently started my talk all over again. At least this time we came to a better conclusion. The manager promised to give us a trial job and test our services. I was happy with being given a trial consignment.

It was the end of the day when I returned to my hotel, and I was tired. I had a shower and then went down to dinner. I had come to understand a few things. In Bombay business was not done the western way, with private meetings according to the clock. Each appointment was very time-consuming, as people had a much more casual approach. You did not talk about business straight away on entering the office. This new way was very different, but I believed in the saying 'when in Rome, do as the Romans do'.

Next day I decided to visit the people I knew in Bombay to find out about Indian thinking, so that I wouldn't start a wild goose chase and waste my visit. I would seek some advice and tips about how to deal with the Indians. Knowing the Indian language and culture was a good start, but it didn't mean I would be successful doing business with them.

As we were a cargo logistics agent doing business on an international level, we had our own cargo agents' network with cities worldwide. My first visit was to our collaborator, the Indian agent in Bombay. The managing director was very happy to meet me. I told him we could work together and organise a joint sales meeting with various importers in Bombay, but they would have to find these importers as they were doing business in the same city.

Our agent was straight with us. He said they were more involved in the export business and did not have any contacts with the importers, so they would not be able to help us. All he could do was offer to check the reputation of any importers I could find. In other words, I was on my own. Usually it is normal practice to work with your agent, to help each other and share the profit.

My next visit was to see Mr Pansari and Mr Choudhary, who were importing their shipments through us. They were very happy to meet me, and offered me lunch at a nearby restaurant. I told them about my experiences and asked how I should handle these matters. They both encouraged me and said I had made the right decision, but said the free import market was relatively new in India and import customs duty was still very high. The Indian government was working on the customs duty sector and had already granted licences to a few import commodities, though the changes would take time.

I asked them what sort of commodities were licensed with reasonable customs duty, and they gave me some useful details about unfinished goods. They could not however provide any sales leads, such as the names of the potential importers.

On my way back to the hotel we got stuck in a traffic jam. I could hear loud music and the beating of drums. I asked the taxi driver what was going on and he said it was the Ganesh Chaturthi festival.

Let me elaborate a little about Ganesh. Ganesh is a Hindu god, the son of Lord Shiva and Parvati, with the body of a human and the head of an elephant. In the Hindu calendar Ganesh Chaturthi falls in August or September. Bombay is the capital of the state of Maharastra, and in Maharastra people worship Lord Ganesh fervently. Some people in South India too worship Ganesh Chaturthi, but it has far more followers in Maharastra.

Ganesh is the lord of success and wisdom, and overcomes obstacles in life. In the Hindu community, whenever someone buys a car or a house or starts a business or anything new in their lives, they pray to a statue of Ganesh. Approximately three months before the start of the celebration, artists make statues of Ganesh of various sizes from about a foot tall up to as much as 20ft. The statues are made of painted clay and are very colourful. The worshipper purchases a statue according to his budget, and these can be very expensive. The statue is taken home and worshipped by family members and friends.

The celebration goes on for eleven days. Each believer decides the exact number of days for which they will say the prayers, and then the statue of Lord Ganesh is taken to a river, a lake or the sea and immersed in water. Along the way the family and their friends can join in the music and dancing, throwing colours in the air on their way to the water. If the statue is small, one of the family carries it on his or her head; if it is too heavy for that, it is carried on a cart or on an open truck while the people walk behind. On the last day, all the statues are immersed and the crowd celebrates the occasion. It is a spectacular festival to watch, but there are many traffic jams during these eleven days of celebrations.

On the third day I set out to visit my remaining three prospects. The third importer was a fair-sized company. By now I knew it was the custom to offer the visitor a glass of water, so I politely refused it, and as before accepted a cup of tea. I had to wait a long time to see the import manager. The receptionist said she knew I must have come from a foreign country. I asked her how she knew, and she said everything about me was foreign. I told her I came from England.

After a while she escorted me in to see the import manager. When he asked me the reason for my visit I came straight to the point, as I could see he was under some sort of pressure. He was polite, but he seemed uncomfortable talking to me. He said he had never heard of my company; he was used to dealing with the big international firms. I gave him my company brochure, and he put it to one side without reading it.

I started my marketing talk by mentioning some big-name clients of ours in other countries. The manager said he would be reluctant to do business with me since he didn't know my company. I argued, but it was in vain. He asked me how he could trust my company, saying their merchandise was very valuable. I had never come across such ridiculous questions and felt very annoyed, but I kept cool. I told him that perhaps it was better that we do business at a later date when he had come to know me. The manager then felt bad that he had offended me and asked me to understand his position.

"Sir I respect what you are saying as you do not know my company, but I must admit I have never came across such suspicious questions from any country I have visited" I replied.

"Please understand, this is India," he said. "You are new here. If you are to do business in India, you must learn." I left the office with goodwill, but my smile was false.

I was very upset about the meeting, as my integrity had been challenged. I did not feel in the right frame of mind to see my other contacts, so I decided to go back to the hotel. Back in my hotel room I telephoned my agent and asked him why he thought I had been given such a reception. He told me not to get upset, because there was much corruption here. Perhaps the man had been hoping for a bribe, and that was why he said, "This is India, you will learn".

I was beginning to realise that besides corruption there was a great deal of suspicion. People would not trust you, and they would keep on asking the same question several times in a different way.

Nevertheless I decided to continue my hunt for business. The next day I set out to tackle the last two contacts. As usual I took the taxi from my hotel. It was the rush hour and the streets were jammed with cars. From my taxi I began to look at Bombay a little differently. At face value it all seemed chaotic – I could see traffic jams on the street, people transporting goods for their customers on handcarts, cars honking even when there was no obstruction. There were always processions, usually wedding participants dancing in the streets or religious followers celebrating some festival. Motor bikes and rickshaws were threading their way through the crowded streets, trying to find gaps between the people and cars. I now saw all of this in a more positive light. Twelve million people were looking for their fortunes in this golden commercial capital of India, and I realised that all these people must be fulfilling their lives every day in their own way. This after all was the reason I had chosen Bombay as the city where I should take the plunge into Indian trade.

The taxi driver somehow found the office of my first contact. When I entered the building the doorkeeper told me the lift was not working. The office was up on the sixth floor, and I was huffing and puffing when I got there; it was a very hot day. There was no receptionist, as the office was small, and there were about fifteen people working away on their own things.

I asked to see the import manager, and a member of staff showed me in to him. It was a very small cubicle, and the manager had an air-conditioning fan behind his chair. The cold air was blowing past him and straight into my face, and it soon became obvious that he had a body odour problem. I was very hot after climbing six floors and felt very uncomfortable.

The manager was on the phone talking to someone, and he had another call waiting. He got up and welcomed me, still on the phone, and pointed to the only chair, which was squashed into the tiny cubicle, and invited me to sit down. I had trouble getting into the chair because of the narrow space. The cold air conditioning was blasting away and I was feeling very uncomfortable sitting there waiting for him.

I waited patiently for about twenty minutes while the manager finished his phone call and then dealt with the second call. He apologised profoundly to me for keeping me waiting. There was a little casual chat and then I started talking business with him. The discussion was a lengthy one, as he had many queries and there was constant interruption from phone calls. He would apologise to me each time, but each time he would take the call. It was obvious that this was a small and very busy company and they were not organised enough to get staff to hold calls while he finished a meeting. I kept cool, but it seemed clear I was wasting my time.

Finally we reached the end of our discussion and the manager said he was very happy with the information I had given him.

"Let's start this new business with an order from Germany" he said. He was giving me a contract! I was astonished and delighted to receive the order. He said that if we did well he would give me three more sectors, the USA, Singapore and Taiwan. I expressed my gratitude to him and promised him good service.

I left the office walking on air. I had been so wrong to underestimate this company, and realised that looks can be deceptive. I checked out their credentials with our agent and he told me the firm was reputable and trustworthy.

My last contact was not available, as the import manager was out of town for a few days, so I took a ride to the Bombay Chamber of Commerce to find out if I could get some sales leads from other potential importers. The office was well organised. They had several files giving information about regular and one-off importers.

I asked them if they would let me sit in their office and make notes, and they agreed. I had found that by and large people in Bombay were very accommodating. They asked for a small fee for the information and I was given a receipt for the money I paid them. It was a very interesting visit, as the details they gave me were exactly what I was looking for. I made a long list of useful addresses and decided to take it with me to England and do a mailshot. Then I returned to my hotel and booked my flight back home the same evening. I felt the market in India was going to be invaluable, but I also knew it would take a long time and lots of hard work. I was determined to do it.

CHAPTER TEN

BREAKTHROUGH

Back home from my first business visit to India, I gave the file I had assembled to the staff in our Uxbridge office and asked them to put all the details in order and create a list for the mailshot, showing air cargo and sea cargo separately.

Our East African business was becoming highly competitive. There were too many new agents in this small market, and profitability was going from bad to worse. However our export and import trade with Mexico, the USA and South East Asia was going well.

We prepared a convincing mailshot for India and mailed some 200 letters to the prospective importers in Bombay. We ended the letter with an important note, saying I wanted to see them soon, as we had wonderful news for them – we could show them how they could increase their profitability.

Meanwhile I made plans for a trip to Lusaka and Ndola in Zambia and Johannesburg and Durban in South Africa. I spent two weeks in southern Africa making joint sales calls with our agents to prospective customers. It was a successful trip.

On my return to England I was surprised to see how many replies we had had from various importers from Bombay who were willing to meet me on my next visit to Bombay. I knew from my last visit that it would be difficult to persuade very big companies to use our services, as the final decision is usually made by more than one CEO, so we had targeted mostly the medium-sized and small companies, as they tended to take decisions quickly. In India the medium-sized companies usually had about 50 to 200 staff and the small companies 10 to 50.

Bombay is a huge city and has many skyscrapers, which made it easy enough to see many people in a small area if you organise the appointments correctly. I decided to get our agent to help me plan the calls, as they knew the city better than me and could advise us on the reputation of each company and the credit facility they would ask from us.

As there are so many religious holidays in India, I had to make sure I chose suitable dates for my visit. My stays were long, so I would always get caught up in one public holiday or another. This time I knew I would be there during Janmashtami, but I thought it would be good for me to take a break and experience this religious festival myself.

I booked in at the same hotel as before and the staff recognised me, so at least I didn't feel a stranger. I rang my agent to say hello. He was happy to hear from me and invited me to dinner with his family. It was a pleasant evening and I enjoyed the dinner. Once again I talked about the possibility of us doing sales calls together, but he was not very interested. He said his staff were not experienced in import marketing as they were very busy with export business. I told him it was a pity he would not be able to share the profits we were going to make, but he was quite happy doing our import clearance only.

Janmashtami is the birthday of Lord Krishna, and the celebration is a unique one. Many boys and girls take part. They form teams, each with their own uniform, usually a T-shirt in the team colour. In the state of Maharastra they celebrate in a different way. In some areas of Bombay, the residents collect money and put it in a clay pot with some milk and butter, as milk and butter was Lord Krishna's favourite. The amount of money can be anything from 5000 to 500,000 rupees.

The pot of money is tied to a rope and the ends of the rope are tied to the second or third floor of the buildings facing each other (Bombay is full of high-rise buildings), so the pot is hanging in the middle of the rope. The teams of boys and girls form human pyramids, and the one on the top of the pyramid has to try to break the pot. Whoever succeeds gets the money.

While they are trying to do this the residents of the buildings throw the water on to them to make it more difficult. It is quite dangerous, as there is no safety net. The participants can fall and are sometimes seriously injured. But it is fun to watch this adventure. While this is all going on there is always music and drums are beaten.

I knew that all importing to India was done on a CIF basis (where the cost of the goods, insurance charges and freight charges are invoiced together by the exporter). This gave me my punchline. When I talked to the importers I would tell them that if they traded on the FOB (free on board) basis instead, they would pay the freight charges themselves. This would save them money, because on the CIF system exporters were taking a profit on the freight charges. This was the approach I had been using in East Africa and it had become very successful. Not only does the importer save money on the freight charges, he has control of the movement of the goods and when the shipment will arrive in India. There was also a saving on customs duty, as the duty was worked out on the value of the goods plus the insurance and freight cost.

I started my visits on a Tuesday morning after making telephone calls to various companies to advise them that I was coming to see them. It was very hot. The traffic was solid and cars were struggling to move forward. Motor bike riders were weaving in between the cars and making more progress than we were. I saw a hilarious scene at one point, when a dog was trying to cross the road. Three times it tried to get across, but the traffic was so dense that it could not find a space and no-one would let it through. In the end the poor animal gave up and went back the way it had come.

I had been told not to encourage beggars on the streets by giving them money, as the beggars were lazy people who didn't want to work and found it an easy way of making money. They were taking advantage of the traffic jam and begging the people in the cars for money.

"Sahib, please don't give money to these people" my driver said. "They know you are a foreigner. They will come from everywhere and bother you."

I had to keep my window open as it was so hot. The beggars were a real nuisance, although I kept looking the other way. At one point I lost my cool and shouted at one of them.

"Please do not shout at me!" he said. "I am not a beggar."

"Then what are you?" I asked him.

"Can't you see, I am working, this is my job!" he said. As the taxi moved forward I could not help laughing.

I arrived at my prospective client's office a little late for my appointment. It was a smart office and many people were working there. The receptionist asked me to sit down and an office boy came with the usual glass of water, which I politely refused. The receptionist said the import manager was very busy, but I could see the assistant import manager. I said I was happy to see the assistant, and she escorted me into a fancy-looking office with quality furniture.

The manager very politely shook hands with me and asked me to sit down. He had two of his other staff present in the office, and for a while we all chatted. As I had come from England the manager was bragging to his colleagues about my visit. I had seen this before with other managers who liked to show off their importance in having contacts with people from foreign countries.

The manager was very curious about me. He asked me a few questions about England and said he had never been to Europe, though he had visited Singapore and Malaysia. He said that they had two offices in Bombay and altogether 450 people worked for the company as well as those in other branches across India. I was impressed.

I started my sales talk. The manager seemed impressed at what I had to say, but he gave me the impression that he was using my talk for his own education rather than listening to me as if I was a prospective supplier. I could clearly see his curious expression.

When he had listened to my free lecture, he said that they had been dealing with the same cargo agent for a long time and he would feel very bad about changing to a new one as they had a very good relationship with the company. I pointed out how much money he would save by doing it my way and offered to prove it by showing the saving I could make on one of his import contracts. He said that the relationship with his supplier was more important than saving money.

"Please try and understand," he said. "One day we might consider asking you to you do the importing for us, but we cannot break this good relationship with your competitor. Please understand our sentiments."

I could not understand these sentiments, as I thought business was about money, but the manager said that that was all he had to say on the matter. I politely told him that one day I would try to convince him, and we shook hands and I left. I felt very disappointed.

When I entered the office of my next prospect I saw that this was another big company, with many people working on one large floor and many cubicles. A young lady escorted me to the office of the import manager.

I could see some machinery parts on display in the glass cabinet in his office, so to make conversation I asked the manager if they were manufactured by his company. He was delighted to show me the parts and explain what they were for. I pretended to take a great interest. He said they were being exported to three European countries, though not to England. They were also importing both by sea and air, mostly from Taiwan and South Korea. These imports were distributed to various traders in India.

Behind his chair there was a handwritten notice with scruffy red writing which said "DO NOT SMOKE AND DON'T EVEN ASK FOR PERMISSION TO SMOKE". I found this very funny.

He asked many questions, such as who else was importing such parts and if they were sold to other countries. I was suspicious about this as these questions had nothing to do with my business, but I was polite. When I asked if he could give me any business, he said no and gave the same reason as my last prospect – sentiment, dedication and so on.

I could see I was not getting anywhere with this client, so I left. I was used to being turned down of course, but in other countries I had worked in it was for the right reasons. As I travelled to my last appointment for the day I was worrying that all these importers would refuse do business with me for sentimental reasons.

The last company was relatively small and had only about 20 staff. I was meeting the managing director, and this time it was a different approach. The managing director referred to my letter, in which I had said I could save them money. I was happy to hear him mention this. I explained in detail how we could save them money, giving him examples and figures. He was very interested, as they were trading on a CIF basis, and gave me the details of an order which had arrived two days before from the USA. He asked me about the savings I could have made for him, and I worked it out. He was shocked to learn how much money he could have saved.

I explained in detail how he should order his goods. The consignment would travel to Bombay at our expense and he would be billed for freighting at a discount rate. We would give him all the flight details and arrival date. On arrival he would pay the agreed freight charges to our nominated agent. The documents would then be given to his firm for them to arrange customs clearance. I told him he was benefiting from the discount because we had a good relationship with the airline, as we gave them lots of business to many destinations worldwide.

The customer was convinced. He agreed to give us business from the USA, Germany and the UK. I went back to the hotel happy, but with a nagging thought – why was the bigger company really giving me such a hard time? Perhaps it was not just sentiment. Perhaps they did not want to change the system because of the amount of work that would be involved, or maybe the manager was taking money under the table from our competitors.

I realised I would have to change my approach right from the start, because once a customer had refused to do business with us it would be difficult to reopen negotiations. I had to take a slightly more aggressive approach, but in a nice way. I thought of trying to contact the managing director, but then he might pass me down to his import manager, whose pride might be hurt that I had tried to go over his head.

I decided that the next time a manager told me he could not trade with me because of his relationship with the existing supplier, I would tell him that I had come all the way from England, that his company had shown an interest in saving money and that if he would not speak to me I would have to go to his managing director.

I began using this new approach the next day. It worked much better, and immediately I started winning clients. When talking to prospects I could now tell them about the companies which had already given us business, and this worked like magic. Whenever possible I would meet my prospects over dinner to get to know them.

Bombay, or Mumbai as it is now known, is a cosmopolitan city and people go there from all over India. It was educational for me to learn how people from different parts of India all had different ways of thinking. I felt that people were thinking in their own language and then translating into English before speaking, and that this meant they would mean slightly different things by the same words.

As I booked for my return flight I was feeling very pleased with my visit. Now I had to wait and see how much business would materialise. I kept in constant contact with my prospective customers to remind them about our company and how keen we were to handle their business. After a short while business slowly started coming in, and within a few months almost all my prospects had started giving us some business.

We now began to get busy, as Christmas was coming. There is a huge population of Christian Indians in India, so Christmas is a national holiday there. Christians in India are very religious and Christmas Day is considered a holy day. They go to church to pray and then to midnight mass. They have a family dinner, with fish instead of turkey as the main meal, and exchange presents. They put up Christmas trees with lights and decorate their homes with colourful lights and decorations, just as we do in England.

As many companies stopped trading just before Christmas and would go on holiday for as long as a month, importers would put in their orders to European suppliers beforehand and all the deliveries would come together to beat the deadline. There was always a problem getting space in the airline or shipping line at Christmas, but somehow we managed it.

I decided to employ a woman who could continue looking after the marketing in my absence and look after our existing customers, as our agent was not very helpful. The agent was however kind enough to provide office space for her.

It was now taking us a long time to get paid, particularly on the larger jobs. Our agent kept coming up with different excuses about the delay. He said the customer was delaying payment to them, creating a knock-on effect.

Early in 1987 I decided to go to Bombay to sort this problem out, as well as to look for more new business. I found that in most cases the agent was being dishonest and was using the money for his benefit. When I decided to put my marketing activities on hold and talk to other agents who were doing similar business with India, I found they all had similar problems with getting paid by their agents in India. Some of them told me scary stories about huge amounts of money that had not been paid.

I had made some good friends in Bombay, and I decided to talk to one of them and tell him about the difficulties I was having. I wondered if it might be better not to do any more business with India. My friend gave me good advice. He said that as long as I depended on agents I would always have problems. It was better to have your own office and your own staff, so you could have direct control.

"Don't go back," he said. "You have already crossed the river, and the grass is definitely greener on the other side. India really is opening its markets and they are much bigger than the East African market."

I took my friend's advice and opened our own company in Bombay, with a small amount of working capital. To open a company there I had to get a chartered accountant to help me to set it up. I was recommended to an accountant, who told me that the rules were different for me because I was British. I needed an Indian citizen to be my partner and take a 60 per cent stake in my company. I told him I did not want to do this, but he said it was the law of the land. I did not believe this, so I went to see a lawyer, but he said the same thing. It did not make sense to me. I felt very frustrated and was not getting anywhere.

I decided to see the Governor of the Reserve Bank of India. I could not get an appointment to see him, so I went without one. When I barged into his office, his secretary told me I had to make an appointment. I was adamant.

"I have come all the way from England," I said. "I will wait here until the Governor is free to see me." The secretary went into the Governor's office, and I was invited in to see him. I explained my position and told him about my frustration and disappointment. He was very apologetic to me for having to go through all these frustrations, and showed me some new rules which had just come into effect. They were designed to encourage non-residents to open businesses independently without Indian partners. He said copies of the new rules had been sent to all parties concerned, but they didn't seem to bother to read them.

The Governor asked me if I now felt ready to start my company, and pointed out some restrictions, which I accepted. I signed a form and he gave me a copy with his signature.

"Give this form to any accountant and he will let you start a company without an Indian partner" he said. It was a great relief for me to win this battle. I went to see another chartered accountant and he arranged to register my company, Courcan Cargo India Pvt Ltd.

Starting a company in India was a big step for me. I began by looking for staff, particularly a manager. Fortunately I had a contact in the UK with a lady who came from Bombay and was working for a cargo agency there. She put me in touch with an Indian called Richard, whom she said was reliable and had a little experience in the industry. I contacted Richard and found he was interested in working for my company as a manager, so I offered him the job.

I decided to rent an office space from a serviced office company. The office was in Vile Parle, a western suburb of Bombay. It was fully furnished, with telephones and other necessary equipment. Richard recommended that we should keep to the bare minimum of one accountant and an office boy, to keep the cost down. The boy would deliver and collect papers and run errands to the bank.

The next day a boy of 16 came to my office looking for a job. His name was Ramu, and I asked him why at his age he was looking for a job instead of going to school.

"I would love to go to school, Sir, but my father is not able to work" said Ramu. "My mother does housework for other people to earn some money. I have a little sister who goes to school. So you can see my mum does not bring in enough money to buy food for our family and for my sister's education. Do you know sir that one day my sister will become a doctor so she can help poor people like us? Sir, please give me a job so we can do all these things and be happy. Our needs are small. I promise you I will be very honest and hard working and I will never ask you for overtime money even if I work after 6 pm. Please sir!"

When I told Ramu I would give him a job he jumped for joy. Then he touched my feet and said "thank you" many times. Touching the feet of the boss or any elder is an Indian custom to show respect. Business people coming from the West for the first time sometimes get the wrong impression when they see a younger host touch the feet of an older Indian guest, but it is simply an old tradition to pay respect to one's elders.

Ramu turned out to be a very hard worker. He was always smiling and nothing was too much trouble for him. He was always keen to know more about our business, and he proved smart and a very quick learner. I also found he had great pride and self respect.

I interviewed a man called Subu for the job of accountant, and he agreed to work for our company. I gave Richard training in management and went with him to see customers whenever I came to Bombay, so that he could look after sales in my absence. I bought a company car for him so that he could visit our customers. After a few days I left for London feeling very satisfied that we now had an office in Bombay, as I felt it had given us the control over our business that would lead to success.

As an Indian born in East Africa I was very different from Indians born in India, but I was learning many good things from them. Indians take a gentle, calm approach to life. To avoid confrontation they will not argue with someone even if they know they are right (which can cause a lot of confusion). They deal with problems with a cool head and are always polite. They respect their elders and have very strong family values.

I found most Indians are very emotional, and by and large they are very religious. They are excellent hosts and give a lot of respect to guests. They have a casual approach towards life and will find time to talk calmly with anybody.

Once I met an Italian agent who came across many Indians in his working life. He said Indians were doing so well in the IT business because they didn't have an aggressive approach to life like us - they were cool and relaxed. I fully agreed with him.

Anyone coming to Bombay for the first time would see the poverty on the streets and think it must be very unsafe, as these poor people might rob us for their survival. Yet by and large the poor people are very contented, because their needs are small. They can live on a small budget as the cost of living is very low. They are also God-fearing people and afraid to harm anyone, because they believe that God will punish them for any wrongdoing.

A businessman told me that thousands of people from small villages and towns came to Bombay every day in search of a better life in this golden city of opportunity. As India progressed, poverty was getting less. "One day all will be well," he said. Today I can already see that things are getting better, as people have been determined to work for a better life.

The negative side of this is that many people have a big ego problem. When they work for a company they want to be called something very important like Managing Director or President - the higher the better. Some Indian employees ask for a glorified title and say they don't even care if there is no more money, it's the title that matters.

Most Indians are very suspicious and don't trust each other until they are absolutely sure of each other. Only when they establish trust in each other do they start doing business.

Visitors from overseas are very well looked after. Their host will personally go to the airport to welcome guests, take them to the hotel and make sure they have a comfortable room. The approach to business meetings is casual to make sure the guest feels at ease.

Since the move towards globalisation, many Indians travelling abroad have complained about the lack of welcome and help they get when they arrive in Western countries. In these countries no-one meets them – they are simply given directions as what to do after arrival at the airport, such as which train to catch, how to get to the hotel and what time to meet at the office.

Thinking about all this on the plane, I got lost in my thoughts. The next thing I knew, the stewardess was waking me to tell me that we would soon be landing at Heathrow and breakfast was being served. I arrived back home very tired and took a day off to recover from the jet lag, because I would soon be leaving for East Africa.

I was beginning to realise that the Indian market had phenomenal potential compared to that in East Africa. After trying to do business in India for a few months I was feeling very frustrated and had lots of negative thoughts, but now our office could barely keep up with the growth. Being very patient in India, and knowing the culture, had paid off.

Indian customers were beginning to come to our office in England, which encouraged me and made me feel we were getting closer to the Indian market and winning the trust of our Indian customers.

Our rented office space was getting overcrowded, and it was very clear by now that we should be expanding. Every day I spoke to Richard by phone about progress in Bombay. I asked him to look for an office with at least 500 square feet of space, and fortunately we soon found a good location near the airport. We bought a small passenger van so that we could take small cargo loads to the airport when necessary.

After visiting Kenya and Tanzania I had to prepare for another trip to India. The next time I landed in Bombay it felt like coming home. Having our own office gave me a lot of confidence and the flow of reports from Richard showed me how fast our business was growing.

Next day I found Richard and the other staff very enthusiastic about the way the business was growing and wanting to take me to meet some bosses of the big companies. I was pleased about this, as we had been concentrating on the small and medium-sized companies. Going to see some of the bigger players made me feel we were getting to a higher level.

We soon won business from one big company, and a second was considering our proposal. Winning a big company's account gave us a lot of encouragement, as we knew we could pull in other companies by mentioning their name. We came up with a new strategy for approaching the big firms, and started getting some big accounts on our books.

I always used to make time to see my regular clients and new prospective customers out of office hours and at the weekend to get closer to them. One customer gave me the name of a man whom he said I should meet; his name was Mr Shah. I phoned him and invited him for dinner at a restaurant, and he said he would like to have dinner at a particular five-star hotel. I told Mr Shah to meet me at the hotel at 7 pm on Saturday. He then asked if he could bring a friend with him. I agreed to this, as I could hardly say no, and we arranged to meet in the bar.

Mr. Shah arrived on the dot of seven and introduced me to his friend, who was called Mr Mehta. He had extraordinarily long teeth, and I couldn't help laughing about them to myself. I imagined that when he came through the main door his teeth must have arrived some time before the rest of his body. I also thought what difficulty he would have with his food.

I soon realised that Mr Shah was wasting my time and my money. He had no intention of doing any business with me. He just wanted an expensive meal at a five-star hotel. At the end of the evening I paid the bill and went home without any business to show for it, but at least I had some laughs thinking about Mr Mehta and his amazing teeth.

One day I accompanied my marketing staff to meet the purchasing manager of a big company with huge offices. We were escorted to an impressive office and introduced to a lady in a sari behind the desk. She noticed my puzzled expression.

"I am the manager," she said. "You look surprised." She was very polite and invited us to sit down. I told her I was very happy to see a lady as the manager of such a huge company and she said there were many women in India who looked after big corporates like this one. I told her how unusual this was in Europe.

I asked her how many staff she had in her department and she said she had 3800 employees. This was a new experience for me, as Europe was still a man's world and nearly all the bosses were male. We thought that all Indian ladies walked behind the man. But later I found that many women in India had senior positions in huge companies.

We soon had to employ more marketing and operations staff to service our growth and give good after-sales service. My stays in Bombay started getting longer, so my wife and I decided to buy an apartment there. We moved there in 1992. We also bought a car, and as I found driving in Bombay impossible we employed a driver, whose name was Anand.

Having our own apartment was a great feeling. This building was in Juju, a western suburb of Bombay. It was near the airport and right on the beach.

We began our new life in Bombay, and were soon making new friends. Ranjna found it difficult to understand the local Hindi dialect, but she made friends in the same building who were happy to go to the market with her to buy fruit and vegetables. She soon picked up the local slang and enjoyed bargaining in the market.

I met a man called Anil living in the same building, and we became very good friends. He often helped me to sort out problems. We all enjoyed going out in the evenings and at weekends, eating out, seeing movies and plays and travelling away to the beautiful mountain areas away from the city.

I soon had an opportunity to meet a wealthy young businessman whose family had a very big apartment all to themselves. He said there were 73 members of the family living there, including his parents, uncles, brothers, cousins and their wives and children and grandchildren. They had only one kitchen and one dining room between them. I asked him how he could possibly handle so many people for dinner.

"Everyone has to come in for dinner on time" he said. "Discipline is controlled by one of the elders."

"Do you sometimes have arguments?" I asked him.

"Yes, but if it goes out of control the elder will tell them to stop it and no-one will talk back. The young ones nowadays do not like the house rules and sometimes they talk back, but always in a polite manner."

I commented that our way of life was changing, and he said that was true, but only in the cities. That sort of unity is rare in big cities, even in India, though it is normal to see such family unity on a smaller scale. In small villages in India such family unity is quite common.

We were settling down into our new life when Richard came to see me one day with a guilty look on his face. In a very low voice he said he had decided to resign from our company. I was shocked and asked him to reconsider his decision. I offered him more money to stay, but he had been offered a job in Dubai and found it very attractive as he was very keen to go abroad. I tried everything to persuade him, but he was adamant.

This was not so surprising. Many young Indians are very keen to leave India and are constantly looking for opportunities to work abroad, particularly in the USA or Europe.

I reluctantly agreed to release Richard. This was very hard for both of us as we had built the company's success in India together. I took over the management and started looking for someone to replace him.

I now started paying attention to the operational side of the business to try to improve our after-sales service. It was traditional in Bombay to send notification that goods had arrived to the customer by post office mail, which would often take five to seven days to get there. Importers were paying a lot of money for a quick delivery service, so to then wait a week for an advice note was ridiculous.

The solution was simple. We told our office boy, Ramu, to deliver all the arrival advice notes himself, the same day or the next, depending on the time of arrival of the flight. The new system worked like magic and the importers were delighted by the quick delivery of our arrival advice notes. We added this service to our marketing presentation, and it encouraged new customers to use our services.

I started looking for a suitable replacement manager, and after a while I managed to find one. The Bombay office continued to bring in more business. As I got a closer grip on the city I began to like it even more.

CHAPTER ELEVEN

TRADE AND TERRORISM

Allow me to start this chapter with a brief history of Bombay, or Mumbai as it is now known. Long ago the city was built on seven islands, which in the 18th century were made into one by reclaiming the land in between. They used to call it the 'golden city', because newcomers found success there, as we did. It was the richest and most populous city in India and offered many opportunities for people to make money. It still does.

Mumbai is the financial capital of India and also the home of the Indian movie industry everyone refers to as Bollywood. Including the movie industry in South India and that in Madras, India makes more movies than any other country in the world.

Mumbai is the liveliest city in India – they say it sleeps for only two hours a day – yet it is also usually very safe. The night life is good, with restaurants representing many international cuisines. There are discos and you see people strolling around on the streets and going for late dinners, including the midnight buffets which are offered by some hotels – they all get packed out.

One day I had an appointment with our chartered accountant in the Fort area of South Mumbai. It was March 12 1993. Mumbai is a very congested city and the Fort area is even worse, as the roads are narrow and traffic is very heavy. Anand, my driver, was having a lot of difficulty getting to the accountant's office. I told him to drop me anywhere and I would walk the rest of the way.

I was talking to my accountant in his office when we heard a tremendous bang. We both jumped in shock. "I have never heard such a loud noise before!" he said. "Something is definitely wrong."

He made a few calls and found that a bomb had gone off in the stock market building, which was very near to his office. Then almost immediately he had a call to say that there had been a second blast.

We all decided to get home as quickly as possible. When I came out on to the street to look for Anand, it was a scene of chaos. People were panicking and running in all directions. Fortunately Anand spotted me in all the chaos. "Let's go quickly, sir!" he said. "There are big problems on the streets." Our apartment was far away on the west side of the city, but Anand knew Mumbai very well. He said he would try getting me home using the back streets.

Everywhere I looked people were running for their lives and cars and motorbikes were being driven very fast. I saw a car burning and people lying on the streets. Some were sitting on the side of the road bleeding from their injuries.

I got into the car, but the traffic was solid. People were shouting and honking, but we could not move. Everybody looked very frightened and some were crying.

Somehow Anand managed to get away from the main roads and into the back streets, but we were still moving very slowly. Normally it took an hour to an hour and a half to get home, but four hours later we were still on the road and had only covered about two thirds of the journey. When we finally got home we had been travelling for six hours. Poor Ranjna was frantic. She had desperately been trying to contact me, but all the phone lines were dead.

"Let's go back to live in the UK!" she said. "I do not want to live here any more" She was in a terrible state. We had a doctor in our building, so we called him and he gave her an injection to calm her down.

The media reported that it had been a terrorist attack by Islamist extremists. There had been 13 bomb blasts in different places across the city. Over 250 people died and more than 700 were injured. Immediately after the bombings there was rioting between Hindus and Muslims and many people from both communities died.

We dusted ourselves down and continued climbing the ladder of success. Encouraged by our customers, I decided to start an office in Delhi. I was already in contact with some people there who were interested in working for us. I asked one of my contacts to do some groundwork and look for an office for us to rent. When he had found a suitable office I went there to see it and to explore the Delhi market. I could see it had great potential, and we started trading there without further ado.

On my way home I always used to see a woman begging by the roadside with a child in her arms. One day I asked the driver to stop the car, and told the woman that if she would come to my house I would give her a job.

"What do you think I am doing now?" she replied. "I make more money begging than you would offer to me."

My driver looked at me. "Sahib, why are you wasting your time with these people?" he asked me. "There are lots of jobs available if you want to work."

I found the business world of Delhi very different to that of Mumbai. Timekeeping was the biggest problem. Companies in Delhi would give us an appointment and then keep us waiting for anything up to two hours. We got round the problem by overbooking appointments. If the customer was not on time we would go to the next appointment and then return for the previous one.

After a few months we started picking up new customers, though by and large I found the business community in Delhi had a less professional approach than Mumbai. We became well known in Delhi, thanks to the marketing presentation we gave, in which we named examples of our clients in Mumbai. This made it easier for us to get customers in Delhi.

The Hindi dialect in Delhi is better and purer than that in Mumbai. In Mumbai they speak a Marathi-based dialect (Marathis are the people of the state of Maharashtra) with many words from Gujarati. People in Delhi do not nod their heads confusingly like people in Mumbai.

Delhi is a well-spread and beautiful city with wide roads, lots of greenery and many old monuments and ancient buildings. The world-famous Taj Mahal is in the city of Agra not far from Delhi and you can get there in three or four hours by road or train. Many businessmen visiting Delhi from overseas go to see the Taj Mahal over the weekend.

I began to recognise the huge magnitude of business in India. The companies were much bigger than I had anticipated. Many people read in the media about the markets of India and China, but now I was beginning to see the true potential for growth.

The weather in Delhi is very cold in winter and very hot in summer. Like Mumbai, Delhi has many huge shopping malls where you can buy anything from a pencil to a car, depending on your budget. They are a shopping paradise.

Our office staff were given sales targets and told to make sure they reached them. I coached them in how to approach prospective customers and other matters.

One Friday evening I decided to take a flight from Delhi to Mumbai. On the way to the airport the taxi got stuck in traffic and was not going anywhere, and I was worried I would miss my flight. My taxi driver got out of the taxi to see what the problem was. He came back to tell me that there was a cow sitting in the middle of the road, so no-one could get past. We both got out and went to see if we could move it.

The cow would not move, so I took a stone to throw at it to try to make it get up.

"Sahib, do not do that," said the driver. "People are watching and they will not like you hitting the cow. It is considered a sacred animal."

I then asked some people to come and help me push the cow away. We all started pushing and in the end we managed to move it to the side of the road.

We managed to get to the airport in time and I boarded the flight. As I was settling into my seat a young sadhu (an Indian holy man) appeared and took the seat next to mine. He was wearing a saffron-coloured cloth and no shoes, and spoke pure Hindi. I greeted him and we started talking.

I found it very strange to see this man, as I had never seen a sadhu on a plane. I asked him why he was not wearing shoes. He said one of his toes was hurting so he had put his shoes in his suitcase. He complained about the airline's service and said he preferred to travel on Jet Airways. He was a very intelligent man, so I enjoyed talking to him and the time passed very quickly.

Saturday is a working day in India, but I decided to stay at home to be with my wife and work from there. We were now well settled in our Mumbai office. There were two rooms, one for me and the other as a general office. The offices were well furnished and custom-designed to be comfortable and spacious.

As I sat doing paperwork in my office, I could hear Subu and Ramu talking in low voices about something. After a while Subu knocked on my door and said Ramu wanted to see me. I asked him to wait a little while as I was in the midst of doing something, and then I called Ramu in. I had great respect for Ramu and his hard work and honesty.

Immediately I could see that something was wrong. Ramu stood by the door, almost hiding from me. I could see only half of him. His eyes were looking at the floor.

"Please sir, may I speak with you?" he asked me in a very low voice.

"What is the matter?" I replied. "Why are you hiding behind the door and looking at the floor instead of coming inside and talking to me as usual?"

"Sir, I am afraid of looking into your eyes," he said. "I am afraid what will happen if you say no to the request I am going to make to you."

"Your behaviour is not right," I said. "You are always very brave and look into my eyes when you talk to me. Come in and talk to me."

I had never before seen Ramu shivering with fear as he was now. He crept into the office and I saw that the corners of his eyes were wet with tears. He was keeping a brave face and trying very hard to stop the tears. He wiped his eyes.

"Look, I am brave, I am not crying" he said.

"I know you are brave and I know you will not cry, Ramu. Please tell me, what do you want?"

"Sir, our little home has a roof of corrugated iron sheet. There are so many holes in our roof and also many other repairs in our little home. The monsoon will start next month. It is very difficult in the rainy season, with rainwater leaking from many places. It is very difficult to sleep at night as we all keep on looking for dry places during the whole night. I wanted to ask you before sir for your help, but I was a new employee, so I decided to prove myself worthy before asking for help. Sir, I never told you this before as I am shy to talk about it, but my father is mentally ill and this is why he cannot help us."

I could not stop the tears coming into my eyes, but I did not want Ramu to see my weakness so I quickly turned my back to him and gathered my composure. I cleared my throat and asked him how much money he needed to repair his house.

Ramu spoke in a trembling voice, scratching his head nervously.

"Sir, I need twenty thousand rupees," he said. This was the equivalent of about £300. I could see the fear on his face in case this request was rejected.

"Don't worry, Ramu," I said. "I will give you the money you need."

Ramu was a very happy young boy. He touched my feet. "Thank you very much sir, and God bless you" he said.

The carpenter who made our furniture was honest and I knew he was looking for work. I sent him to Ramu's home to see that the job was done properly. A few days later Ramu came to our office with his sister Savita.

"Remember I told you about my sister?" he asked me. "Now she can speak English." Savita looked at me and said "Good morning Sir".

"You see," said Ramu. "Savita can speak English, but I told her not to speak too much to my boss because he is very busy and you should have respect not to speak too much in front of him."

Savita looked shyly at Ramu. "Ramu, I respect you also," she said. "May I go home now please?"

The continuous growth in the company also brought growth to our senior staff, both in Mumbai and Delhi. The senior personnel were given company cars. Most of our staff were young and very enthusiastic – surprisingly enough, 75% of the Indian population are 25 years old or younger, and they represent the future of India. Our staff were always on the go, looking for further growth. Almost everyone was working late in the office to accommodate the different time zones of other countries we were dealing with.

All the employees would bring their own food in a box from home, and at lunchtime they would all sit together and share.

As an example of a logistics company with a new and original way of working, I would cite the case of the dabbawala service. A dabbawala (it means literally a 'box carrier') collects fresh food in a dabba (box) from the employee's home each day and takes it to his or her office. All the dabbas look the same and most employees cannot read, yet they are all delivered to the right address. The charge used to be just one rupee per day, not much more than a British penny, but two million meals a day were delivered, all without a computer system, and they don't make mistakes.

India has many festivals, mostly connected to some religious event and usually celebrated with great happiness. In March there is the colourful festival of Holy. When it was time to celebrate Holy, our neighbour asked us to join them in the compound of our apartment building. We knew what Holy was all about – everyone, from children to old people, takes part and they all throw coloured water or powder on each other, dance and enjoy the music and have a late lunch.

We all arrived at the compound in the morning and started throwing coloured powder and water at each other. It was great fun. After a while one we could no longer recognise each other, as everyone's face and clothes were saturated with colour. We all enjoyed the day, but we soon found that the colours could not be washed off, particularly from our hair. Some people had not played by the rules, as you are not supposed to use permanent colours.

The next day I was flying to London for a meeting with my bank manager to ask him for a loan. I tried all sorts of things to get rid of the colour from my hair, but it was no good – I would have to wait for it to grow out.

When the bank manager saw me with my hair bright yellow and red, his jaw dropped and his eyes popped almost out of his head.

"Oh my god, Sam!" he said. "Is this a new style, or are you becoming a punk?" I was embarrassed, but I turned it into a joke, and explained the Holy festival to him. I told him I would not be taking part in it again. He could not help staring at my hair every now and again as we talked, but at the end of our discussion he approved the loan I wanted.

Back in Mumbai our staff were working in a very restricted office space as we took on more and more staff to deal with the growth of the business. I decided to find an additional office so that we could all work in comfort. We were lucky, as we found a suitable new building not far from our existing office and very close to the airport.

Now that we had premises in Mumbai and Delhi our customers were asking us to open branches in Madras and Bangalore as well, so that they could have similar services in those cities under one organisation. We decided to open an office in Madras first and then one in Bangalore.

 One day I was travelling in a taxi from Madras airport to the hotel. I was used to speaking Hindi with everyone, so I told the taxi driver in Hindi to take me to the Taj Connemara hotel. The taxi driver turned to look at me.

"That is the language of Delhi, not Madras," he said. "But I will take you to the hotel."

"But you do understand Hindi?" I said.

"Yes, a little, but in Madras you speak Tamil, not Hindi" he said.

"I don't speak Tamil," I said.

"Then please speak English," he said.

I admired the courage and pride the man was showing in his Tamil language, but I also thought he was being aggressive and rude to his passenger. I decided to ignore him, and continued to speak Hindi.

I studied the market in Madras and found it was an important city of Tamil Nadu, in the south east of India. In Madras, when you go and meet the customer, they don't offer you water or tea as they do in other cities.

The seaport of Madras helped us from the logistics point of view. Mumbai was feeding the western Indian market, Delhi was feeding the north and Madras was looking after the south. In this way we could cover most of India, though there were still some areas where we needed to open more offices to complete the picture. As usual we employed the basic staff for the Madras office, with the same strategy of working as in our Mumbai and Delhi offices. Our growth continued and over the years we opened offices in Bangalore and some satellite offices in Southern India.

One day I was travelling in a rickshaw in Bangalore; it was the end of the day and I was going back to my hotel. When we arrived at the hotel, I asked the driver how much the fare was. He looked at the meter.

"Is it OK for you to pay me the amount on the meter?" he asked.

"Of course it is," I said. "Why are you asking me?"

"I mean are you happy to pay the amount according to the meter?"

"I am happy, but it is very unusual to ask such a question."

"Sir, if you are not happy then you do not have to pay me. I am a Christian and people travelling in my rickshaw should be happy. If they are happy then God will be happy too."

I told him this was the wrong way to run the business. If he was providing a service he was entitled to his due reward. I paid the fare and went into the hotel thinking that this was the most unusual rickshaw driver I had ever come across.

Gujarat, the state to the north of Mumbai, was now becoming a huge growth area, and we opened offices in Ahmadabad and Baroda. I was kept very busy travelling to all our branches as well as flying back to the UK to visit our office there.

It was important to keep the focus on India, as growth was so fast. All our branches in India were proving successful, and each management team was working independently to build the business. It was all going very well.

CHAPTER TWELVE

FAREWELL TO INDIA

One day in early March 1997 I flew to Britain to visit our UK office. I was working with Ranjna in the office, and the weather was chilly so the heating was on. Suddenly I started perspiring and feeling hot. I was feeling very uncomfortable and could not breathe, so I went into the warehouse next door, as I knew it would be cooler there.

After a while I felt a little better and came back into the office. Ranjna saw that I was still sweating, and knew that something must be seriously wrong. She called an ambulance and I was taken to Hillingdon hospital nearby.

At the hospital they carried out some tests and found I had had a heart attack. They immediately admitted me. After a few days they transferred me to Harefield Hospital, Middlesex, which specialises in heart surgery. The doctors decided to do an angiogram to examine my arteries and if possible unblock them using a stent to improve the blood flow to my heart.

I was hoping and praying that they would be able to unblock my arteries so that I could go home within a day, but I was not that lucky. The surgeon told me I was going to need open-heart surgery, as seven of my arteries were blocked. I was petrified at the prospect of having such a big operation and broke down crying. Why was this happening when everything else in my life was going so well? Ranjna was very strong. She kept on comforting me and giving me courage.

The surgery was carried out and afterwards I had to spend two days in intensive care because there were complications. Finally I was put back on the ward. I spent a few more days recovering and was then allowed back home. It was not for several more months that I was sufficiently recovered to travel to India again.

My staff in Mumbai were very happy to see me back in the office. The manager assured me that all was well and I should not worry, because they would continue taking care of the company. I thanked him and the rest of the staff for looking after everything in my absence.

After this I decided to sell our UK organisation so that I could give my full attention to our Indian offices. In 1999 I finally managed to sell the UK office.

I was now based in our Mumbai headquarters, but our worldwide agency network kept me very busy travelling. Our overseas agents were regularly visiting our offices to arrange joint sales to various customers.

I maintained my relationship with our staff at all levels. The management teams were given the freedom to run their own branches and make sure business kept growing continuously. The infrastructure and distribution system were running like clockwork.

One day Ramu asked my secretary if he could talk to me in private. I made time free for him. Like most of our staff, he was dedicated to his work. I knew he was getting more and more involved in our business and also managing to learn English from our staff without disturbing them in their work.

In came Ramu. "Sir" he said. "I have already paid back almost all the money you lent me. But Sir, I need some more money, can you please help me again?"

"Why do you need the money?" I asked him.

"My mum wants my sister Savita to get married and I need a loan of thirty thousand rupees." I told Ramu that this was a lot of money and asked him how he could pay me back. 30,000 rupees was the equivalent of about £450.

Ramu said he would pay back 70 percent of his salary over the next two years. I told him that if he did this it would be impossible for his family to live. I suggested that the company could give the money as a wedding gift for Savita, so he wouldn't have to worry about paying it back.

Ramu looked at me. "Sir, please forgive me but I will not accept charity" he said. "I will work hard and pay it back. Please let me live with my dignity."

I agreed to lend the money to Ramu, and he was very happy and grateful. I told him that he should get married at the same time, so it would work out better for him. He quickly answered that he was going to do this anyway. He showed me a picture of his fiancée. He invited me to the double wedding, but I could not attend as I was away on business.

I told my accountant to increase Ramu's salary to a much better level so that he could pay back the company without suffering. This was a better way of giving him the money, because his pride would not be hurt.

When Ramu saw his pay packet, he came to see me. He had an innocent, puzzled look on his face.

"Sir" he said. "Why am I paid so much money? I am not due an increase for another eight months!"

"We are promoting you to senior office boy" I told him. "You will also do some clerical work, since you can write a little English." He was very happy and grateful.

Back in England my mother was now 89 years old. I had always loved my mum. She was always there to do all she could for us four brothers, so I wanted to do my best for her. She had always enjoyed a good healthy life and had kept very active, but now I could see that her health was declining.

My wife and I were very close to my mother, so now that we had moved to India we asked her to come and live with us there. She would be better looked after in Mumbai, as we had servants. But she would not come to India. She was very independent and had lived in England for a long time. She also had many friends there.

I was very worried about her health, so I suggested she should move into a nursing home. She agreed to this, on condition that the home was in the Wembley area where her friends were living. With great difficulty I managed to get her a place in a nursing home in Wembley and she was happy to move there. However her health kept on declining. My wife and I were flying back and forth between Mumbai and England to spend as much time as we could with her.

On a visit to England in 2000, Ranjna and I found that Mum's breathing problem was going from bad to worse. We had been experiencing a lot of stress in India and needed a break, so we had arranged a week's holiday in Interlaken in Switzerland. We were now very worried about my mum's condition and were prepared to cancel our holiday, but she insisted we should go.

While we were in Switzerland my wife was feeling very uneasy, so she phoned Shashi to ask how Mum was. He told us she had passed away just a few hours earlier.

We were both totally devastated, and felt extremely guilty for having taken our holiday. We immediately took the train to Zurich for the flight to London. All the time we were crying and trying to comfort each other. My guilt over not having been with my mum when she died will always stay with me.

People in Mumbai usually love the monsoon season, which runs from about the middle of June to the end of September. They appreciate the wet weather because it is so cooling and refreshing after the heat of summer. The residents are happy to see rain and enjoy walking in it. In the low-lying areas it is common to see flooded streets, and the water may be three feet deep.

On July 26 2005 we were all busy working in the office when the rain started pouring down more heavily than usual. One of the staff came to my office on the third floor.

"Sir, we all have to go home!" he said. "We have never seen rain as heavy as this before." I looked outside and saw water starting to pour through a broken gutter. The lift was not working, so we all tried to get down the stairs. We had to be very careful, as the stairs were like a waterfall. When we finally arrived on the ground floor the water was almost two feet deep.

I have never seen such heavy rain in my life. It was falling in sheets. My wife and I got into our car and we set off into the torrential rain. Our driver could hardly see through the windscreen and could only drive very slowly.

The driver tried several ways to get us to our home in Juhu, but we were blocked at every turn by the fast-moving water. It was up to six feet deep in places. There was no help from the police or fire brigade. All the mobile phones had stopped working, so there was no way we could contact our maid or our neighbour to tell them what was happening. We did meet some young boys and girls who volunteered to guide us – they told us to go back, as some cars had already been submerged by the floods.

As we drove we started to see bodies floating in the floods, people who had not been so lucky as us. It was truly terrible.

I told the driver to head towards the airport, as it was on higher ground and we might find accommodation in a hotel there. Six hours later, after a great struggle, we finally got to the ITC Sheraton hotel. The hotel lobby was full of people like us trying to get rooms. There were not enough rooms of course, and some were sleeping in the lobby.

My wife was not feeling well after our ordeal and she was finding it difficult to breathe. We pleaded with the receptionist, who took us to one side. She said she had one room, but it did not have air conditioning. We took the room anyway.

We were both drenched from head to foot, so we dried ourselves as well as we could. We were hungry, so we went to the coffee shop for a meal before going to bed.

Next day we hoped to go home, but we were told that the water was still very high near our home. We had no choice but to go back to the hotel and stay another night.

July 26 2005 turned out to be the wettest day in the city's history - 39 inches of rain had fallen in 24 hours. At least five thousand people drowned in the floods and many more went missing. Thousands of animals died and sewage works overflowed. It was a dreadful time. No warning had been given by the met office that such unusual rainfall was on the way.

Since all the management teams were now running their branches independently and successfully, I started reducing my day-to-day activities in the company. I was now 65 years old and was thinking of retirement. Our sons Sohail and Sunil had both now settled in Canada. We invited Sohail, as our elder son, to come to India and take over the business, but he did not want to take up this offer as he had other problems to think about and wanted to stay in Canada. I did not ask Sunil as he was busy with his own affairs.

My wife and I decided to sell the business and retire. We found a European logistics company who were interested, and in 2005 they bought us out.

There was a transition period while we handed over the company to the new owner. We were running the company like a big family, so it was very difficult to tell our staff that we were selling up. We knew they would be very upset, as Ranjna and I were like parents, particularly to all the young staff. We had to break the news gently. They all took it well except, of course, Ramu. He came to see me at my home, weeping loudly and begging me not to sell.

"We all need you to continue being our father and our boss!" he sobbed.

"Ramu!" I said. "Please stop crying. You have made good progress in your life. You are earning good money and you have two wonderful children. You will have very good bosses, and they have promised not to change anything, so you can all live happily. Now I am old and wish to enjoy the rest of my life, so please try to understand and have consideration for me and my wife."

Ramu looked at me with sad eyes, but his expression was sympathetic. "Sir, god bless you both, and you both deserve a happy and a healthy life" he said. Today Ramu is fully-grown up and working his way up in the company.

Western governments keep on putting pressure on the Indian government to make children go to school. They are right to say that all children should go to school and there should not be child labour. There are many Ramus in India, boys who lost their childhood and took the responsibility to look after their families at a very early age, through no fault of their own.

There had been another terrorist attack in Mumbai in 2006, when extremists planted bombs on commuter trains, killing more than 200 people. On November 26 2008 they struck a third time. Ranjna and I arrived from London to be met as usual by our driver Babu. He said there had been an outbreak of shooting in South Mumbai, and people were panicking. As we drove home we saw a car outside a hotel, blown up like the ones I had seen during the 1993 attack. The streets were empty, and we were home in 20 minutes. As soon as we were inside I switched on the TV to see what was happening, but the service had been cut off as we had been away for several months.

We were both very tired and went to bed. The following morning our TV service had been restored and we sat down to watch the news.

All the channels were full of the story. There had been about 10 co-ordinated attacks across the city, and terrorists, apparently from Pakistan, had taken over the Taj Hotel, where we had stayed on our first visit to India, and the Oberoi. People staying in the hotels had been taken hostage and some had been killed. The local police could not handle such a situation, so they had called in trained commandos from the National Security Guard, but these men had to come from Delhi and it would take time for them to get to Mumbai.

Meanwhile the hotels were under siege. The police were trying their best to rescue people from the hotel, but some police officers were killed by the terrorists.

When the commandos arrived the next day they knew how to handle the situation. They mounted what was called Operation Black Tornado. They managed to kill all the terrorists except one, who went on a shooting rampage at the railway station. Eventually he was caught by a police officer and he is still in jail for his crimes. He admitted that the terrorists were from a Pakistan-based terrorist organisation.

It was shocking to see all this on our arrival in Mumbai. A couple of days later we took a ride in our car to see the hotels, but we were not allowed inside.

There were many dreadful stories about what had happened. A woman journalist had been staying on the sixth floor of the Taj. Having heard gunshots, she rang her husband on her mobile to tell him what was happening. As she was talking two terrorists broke into her room. She got under the bed to hide, but they found her. Her mobile was still connected and her husband heard the two gunshots as they killed her.

The manager of the Taj and his family were staying on the same floor and his wife and children were killed in their hotel room while he was out of the room. The terrorists killed customers in a restaurant in the city called the Leopold, which is very popular with tourists. In all more than 160 innocent people had been slaughtered.

I feel so much can be done both by East and West to improve relations, as we need each other. There are many opportunities for the western world to do business with India. A very large proportion of the Indian population are between the ages of 25 and 30, and they are very keen to make progress for themselves and their country. The opportunity is much greater than people realise.

Most westerners are disciplined, whereas for Indians everything is negotiable. The two communities have to understand each other better and meet halfway. That will bring progress on both sides.

The strong economy and progress of India has created many new millionaires. I have seen wealth spreading to the middle classes and poorer classes too. Quality of life is improving for everyone. You don't see as many beggars these days. The ones you do see you may often be seen talking on their mobile phones! Of course, all this rapid progress does have a downside - corruption is also on the increase.

I will relate one story from my personal experience. One day I was standing on the pavement waiting for someone. On the opposite side of the road I saw a lady sitting on the pavement with a boy and a girl. The boy was about four years old and the girl no more than about two. They had a small saucepan with a little food in it. The boy was eating and the girl was crying and shouting to her brother to give her some of the food. But the boy finished the food and put the saucepan down upside down.

The little girl kept on crying and asking for food, and the mother was trying to keep her quiet. I felt so sorry for them that I crossed the road and offered the mother 100 rupees.

"Sahib, hame paisa mat do hum bhikari nahi hai!" she said - do not give money to us, we are not beggars.

There are many poor people who will not beg because they want to work for their living, but in a city like Mumbai, where rents are high, newcomers have no choice but to live on the pavement or in a slum.

India needs a better infrastructure to cope with the fast-increasing traffic. The environment is getting better, but only very slowly. Growth is very fast, and the Government cannot keep up. Property prices, particularly in Mumbai, are extremely high and the cost of living is getting higher by the day.

Many people come to India to save money on medical treatment. They should think carefully before choosing a GP or a dentist. Many of them are more interested in making money than doing their jobs well. There are many good doctors, surgeons and hospitals in the big cities, but you have to do your homework to find them.

Many cities have changed their names back to the original Indian names. After Bombay became Mumbai in 1995, Madras became Chennai in 1996 and Bangalore became Bangluru in 2006.

Most big cities have good road systems and excellent distribution systems – the railway network in India is probably the largest in the world. The telephone system is much better than it used to be. The shopping malls have all the international brands as well as local upmarket brands. There are now more middle-class people in India, and the gap between rich and poor has closed. Generally, lifestyles in India are much better than they used to be.

When I first decided to set up a business in India, my East African Indian friends all tried to discourage me and tell me I was wasting my time and money, because India was the most difficult country to do business in and many East African Indians had failed there. It is true that East African Indians and native Indians don't see eye to eye and there is a huge cultural difference in their thinking. Perhaps the only common factor is their language.

Some of my East African friends told me that my poor education would hinder my progress in India. My reply was "Either you are rich in education or rich in money". I have found that it is rare to see a rich man who is highly educated; educated people tend to be too calculating and cautious about taking risks.

Now I am happily retired. Thanks to my experience in three countries – Africa, England and India – I am able to act as a business consultant.

Even today I would never live in an isolated residence anywhere; my past experiences have left a scar which will never go away.

I came to India determined to make a go of it. I became part of Indian society and was well accepted. I loved India, and believe it has a great future. By and large Indians are calm people, sharp in thinking, patriotic, helpful and have very good memories. I was puzzled that when I first arrived in India people knew immediately that I was from overseas, but after living there for more than 20 years my wife and I can now also see the difference between local Indians and those from abroad.

Today England is our home, and Ranjna and I are well accepted in English society. Our sons in Canada have tried to persuade us to go and live there, but we both love England and cannot imagine settling down anywhere else.

My friends tell me I have had an unusual life. When I think of all that has happened to me and the good and bad things I have seen in three great countries, I have to agree with them.

THE END